THE REFINEMENT OF SOULS

THE REFINEMENT OF SOULS

A translation of

تاج العروس الحاوي لتهذيب النفوس

Tāj al-'arūs al-ḥāwī li-tahdhīb al-nufūs

Imam Ibn 'Aṭā' Allāh al-Sakandarī

SECOND EDITION

Translated by
Amjad Mahmood

HERITAGE
PRESS

The Refinement of Souls: A Translation of Tāj al-'arūs al-ḥāwī li tahdhīb al-nufūs

Published by: Heritage Press
First Edition Published in: April 2014/Jumādā al-Ākhir 1435
Second Edition Published in: October 2016/Muḥarram 1438
This edition revised in: March 2019/Rajab 1440
Website: www.heritagepress.co.uk
E-mail: info@heritagepress.co.uk

Author: Imam Tāj al-Dīn Ibn 'Aṭā' Allāh al-Sakandarī
Translation: Amjad Mahmood

A catalogue record of this book is available from the British Library.

ISBN: 979-8-4579675-5-7

Typeset by: nqaddoura@hotmail.com
Cover design by: Qutaiba al-Mahawili

Contents

Transliteration Key

ء	' (A distinctive glottal stop made at the bottom of the throat.)
ا	*a*, *ā*
ب	*b*
ت	*t*
ث	*th* (Pronounced like the *th* in *think*.)
ج	*j*
ح	*ḥ* (Hard *h* sound made at the Adam's apple in the middle of the throat.)
خ	*kh* (Pronounced like the *ch* in Scottish *loch*.)
د	*d*
ذ	*dh* (Pronounced like the *th* in *this*.)
ر	*r*
ز	*z*
س	*s*
ش	*sh*
ص	*ṣ* (An emphatic *s* pronounced behind the upper front teeth.)
ض	*ḍ* (An emphatic *d*-like sound made by pressing the entire tongue against the upper palate.)
ط	*ṭ* (An emphatic *t* pronounced behind the front teeth.)
ظ	*ẓ* (An emphatic *th*, like the *th* in *this*, made behind the front teeth.)
ع	' (A distinctive Semitic sound made in the middle of the throat, sounding to a Western ear more like a vowel than a consonant.)
غ	*gh* (A guttural sound made at the top of the throat, resembling the untrilled German and French *r*.)
ف	*f*
ق	*q* (A guttural *k* sound produced at the back of the palate.)
ك	*k*
ل	*l*
م	*m*
ن	*n*
ه	*h*
و	*w*, *u*, *ū*
ي	*y*, *i*, *ī*

Introduction

In the name of Allah, the All-Merciful, the Compassionate. All praise is due to Allah, and may His blessing and peace be upon our master Muhammad, his family and Companions.

Allah ﷻ says, 'And by the soul, and the proportion and order given to it; and its enlightenment as to its wrong and its right. Truly, he succeeds who purifies it, and he fails who corrupts it!' (Qur'an 91:7–10).

This short work is a translation of the widely acclaimed Sufi treatise *Tāj al-'arūs al-ḥāwī li tahdhīb al-nufūs* [The bride's crown: comprising the souls' refinement], by the great gnostic and scholar of Egypt, who needs no introduction, Imam Ibn 'Aṭa' Allāh al-Sakandarī رحمه الله. The work, as suggested in its title, addresses the topic of refinement and purification of the human soul through repentance from the inner and outer sins, struggling against the lower self and treating spiritual ailments like conceit, envy and pride, amongst many others. The exposition is articulated by means of counsels and admonishments that have been beautifully expressed in verses of the Qur'an, Prophetic sayings, similitudes and anecdotes of Sufi saints. Although the treatise was authored several centuries ago, it is as if the author is addressing the public in our time, as the same spiritual diseases that existed in his era are also prevalent, even more so, in ours.

The book is not an abstruse esoteric Sufi work whose benefit only extends to an elect few, but is rather a practical manual on purification of the self that serves both Sufi and non-Sufi aspirants alike, both the beginners and advanced seekers on the spiritual path, written by a master who himself was realised in the higher spiritual realities and whose heart and soul was illumined. Just as the crown is an adornment for a bride by which her beauty is enhanced, similarly the refinement of the soul is its adornment by which its beauty is made manifest.

The following editions were relied on for this translation:

- Maktabah Ibn al-Qayyim, Damascus, Syria, 1419/1999. It was edited by Muḥammad 'Alī Muḥammad Baḥrī and Khālid Khādim al-Sarūjī, who relied on a manuscript edition in al-Asad Library and four other editions prevalent in book markets.
- Maktabah 'Ilm al-Ḥadīth, Damascus, Syria, 1420/2000. This edition was edited by Shaykh Yūsuf ibn Maḥmūd al-Ḥāj Aḥmad and revised by the late Ḥanafī jurist and theologian of Damascus Shaykh Adīb al-Kallās رحمه الله.

The subject headings found throughout are not from the original work, but have been included, though occasionally amended, from two Egyptian editions: Dār Jawāmi' al-Kalim, Cairo, 1425/2004 and al-Maktabah al-Azhariyyah li al-Turāth, Cairo, 1429/2008.

I would like to thank: Shaykh Maḥmūd Miṣrī, for providing clarification on a few passages (which I have included as footnotes beginning with '[SM]'); Andrew Booso, for editing; Muhammad Ridwaan, for proofreading; Qutaiba al-Mahawili, for the cover design; and Abdassamad Clarke and Naiem Qaddoura, for typesetting.

Author's biography[1]

His name, lineage and life

He is Imam Tāj al-Dīn, Abū al-Faḍl and Abū al-'Abbās, Aḥmad ibn Muḥammad ibn 'Abd al-Karīm ibn 'Abd al-Raḥmān ibn 'Abd-Allāh ibn Aḥmad ibn 'Īsā ibn al-Ḥusayn ibn 'Aṭā' Allāh al-Judhāmī.[2] His exact date of birth is unknown.

The author's life can be divided into three phases. The first is his early life in the city of Alexandria in the second half of the seventh century Hijri. It was during this period that he studied the Islamic sciences such as *tafsīr*, hadith, *fiqh*, and the linguistic sciences of grammar, morphology and rhetoric under the most eminent scholars of Alexandria. In this early phase, he was severely critical against the Sufis.

The second phase of his scholarly journey is defined by his companionship of the spiritual mentor Abū al-'Abbās al-Mursī, under whom he received his Sufi training in the Shādhilī Order. This was after his encounter with the shaykh and subsequently realising that accompanying the Sufis does not necessarily mean abandoning the pursuit of seeking knowledge or any other worldly pursuits as long as Allah's countenance is sought thereby.

---

1. The following biographical details have been largely, although not exclusively, selected from the various relied-upon editions of the author's works, which have been referenced throughout this work.

2. An ascription to Judhām, a well-known Arab tribe from the Ḥijāz; his forefathers were from this tribe who had migrated to Egypt and settled in Alexandria after the Islamic conquest of Egypt.

Before meeting his spiritual mentor Shaykh Abū al-'Abbās al-Mursī, he had a confrontation with one of Shaykh Mursī's students, which he relates in his work *Laṭā'if al-minan*, 'Regarding him [Shaykh Mursī], I used to condemn and object, not because I had heard anything objectionable from him or something that was authentically reported to me about him, but because of a dispute that took place between me and one of his students, and that was before I accompanied him. I said to that man, "There is nothing but outer knowledge, and these people [Sufis] claim extraordinary matters which the apparent meanings of the Sacred Law openly rejects." The reason for my encounter with him was that, after the dispute that took place between me and that man, I said to myself, "Let me go and see this man, for someone who is truthful has signs that are not hidden." So I attended his gathering and found him speaking with words enjoined by the Shariah that sooth the hearts (*anfās*); [for example,] he said, "...the first is Islam, the second is *īmān* [faith], and the third is *iḥsān* [perfection]; and if you wish, you can say, 'The first is Shariah [Sacred Law], the second is *ḥaqīqah* [reality], and the third is *taḥaqquq* [realisation].'"' He further said, 'I realised that this man is drawing from the vastness of the divine ocean and the lordly succour, so Allah removed from me my scepticism.'[3] He thereafter became one of his elite disciples and closely accompanied him for twelve years, until his lights shone on him and he received spiritual unveilings at his hands.

The third phase begins after his shaykh, Abū al-'Abbās al-Mursī, passes away and he becomes the inheritor of his knowledge and the propagator of his path. He then leaves Alexandria and takes up residence in Cairo, where he becomes busy teaching Islamic law and Sufism, and sermonising in the most prestigious and greatest Islamic university of the time: al-Azhar. It is in Cairo that this phase ends with his death in 709 AH. This phase

3. Muḥammad ibn 'Abbād, *Sharḥ al-Ḥikam al-'Aṭā'iyyah* 1st edition. (Damascus: Dār al-Farfūr, 1423/2003), 44.

is distinguished by his maturity and proficiency in Islamic law and Sufi knowledge, and his benefiting others in these two fields by way of teaching and sermonising.

His school of thought

Imam Tāj al-Subkī says that he was a Shāfi'ī in Islamic law, though other scholars are of the opinion that he was a Mālikī.

His shaykhs

He studied under the foremost scholars of his time, amongst them:

- Shaykh Shihāb al-Dīn Aḥmad al-Abraqūhī, the *Musnid* of Egypt;
- Shaykh Muḥyī al-Mārūnī, under whom the author studied Arabic grammar. Al-Mārūnī was considered on a par with the grammarian Ibn al-Nuḥḥās;
- al-Ḥāfiẓ Sharaf al-Dīn al-Dimyāṭī, who was the shaykh of the hadith experts (*muḥaddithīn*);
- Shaykh Muḥammad ibn Maḥmūd, commonly known as Shams al-Dīn al-Aṣfahānī, who was an Imam [authority] in logic, theology, principles of jurisprudence and polemics. It is most likely that the author studied under him the principles of jurisprudence, theology and the rational sciences such as philosophy and logic.

His most prominent students and disciples

Many renowned scholars benefited from him, amongst them were:

- the shaykh of the Shāfi'īs, Imam Taqī al-Dīn al-Subkī (father of Tāj al-Dīn al-Subkī, the author of *Ṭabaqāt al-Shāfi'iyyah al-kubrā* [The greatest compendium of the

Shāfi'ī jurists]), who was the most prominent of his students;

- Shaykh Dāwūd ibn 'Amr, more well known as Ibn Bākhilā, who was Ibn 'Aṭā' Allāh's successor in the Shādhilī Order;
- Shaykh Abū al-Ḥasan 'Alī al-Qarāfī.

His acclaimed works

The Imam wrote many works, predominantly on Sufism; some of which are:

- *al-Ḥikam al-'Aṭā'iyyah* ['Atā's aphorisms]; it is his most celebrated and acclaimed work, on which many succeeding scholars from all schools of thought wrote commentaries and which is still today taught and memorised in Islamic institutes in the Muslim world;
- *al-Tanwīr fī isqāṭ al-tadbīr* [Illumination in renouncing planning];
- *Tāj al-'arūs al-ḥāwī lī tahdhīb al-nufūs* [The bride's crown: comprising the souls' refinement], which is the current work;
- *Laṭā'if al-minan fi manāqib al-Shaykh Abī al-Ḥasan wa tilmīdhihī al-Shaykh Abī al-'Abbās al-Mursī* [Subtle blessings on the virtues of Shaykh Abū al-Ḥasan [al-Shādhilī] and his disciple Shaykh Abū al-'Abbās al-Mursī].

His miracles

Kamāl ibn al-Humām[4] visited his grave ﷺ and began reciting *Sūrah al-Hūd*, until he reached the verse 'Of those (gathered) some

4. He was a major Ḥanafī jurist from Egypt, most famous for his commentary on the Ḥanafī classic *al-Hidāyah*, titled *Sharḥ Fatḥ al-Qadīr*. He passed away in Ramadan in 860 AH in Cairo and was buried close to the author in the same graveyard.

will be wretched and some will be felicitous' [Qur'an 11:105], whereupon he responded from his grave with a loud voice, 'O Kamāl, there is no one amongst us who is wretched.' Consequently, Kamāl left a will that he be buried there after he dies.[5]

One of his disciples performed the hajj and saw the shaykh in the *maṭāf* area [around the Kaaba], behind the Maqām [the standing place of Ibrāhīm], in the Sa'ī area and in 'Arafah. When he returned to Egypt, he enquired about the shaykh and if he had left the country in his absence for hajj? They replied, 'No.' Then the shaykh entered and greeted him and asked, 'Who did you see during this journey of yours?' He replied, 'My master, I saw you.' So he smiled and said, 'A great man fills the world. If the Quṭb was invited from a hole, he would respond.'[6]

What scholars have said about him

His shaykh, Abū al-'Abbās al-Mursī, said to him, 'Adhere [to the path], for by Allah, if you adhere, you shall be a mufti in the two schools of thought.' In other words, he would thus master the school of the people of Shariah (outer Islamic sciences) and the school of the people of *ḥaqīqah* (namely, the inner sciences). And he said about him one day, 'This young man will not die until he becomes a propagator, calling people to Allah's path.'

Imam Sha'rānī said about him, 'The great abstinent admonisher, the disciple of Shaykh Yāqūt, and before him Shaykh Abū al-'Abbās al-Mursī. He would benefit people through his *ishārāt* [subtle allusions]. People's souls would find His speech sweet and awesome.'[7]

---

5. al-Munāwī, *al-Kawākib al-durriyyah* (Beirut: Dār al-Ṣādir, 1420/1999), 3:10.

6. *Ibid.*

7. 'Abd al-Wahhāb al-Sha'rānī, *al-Ṭabaqāt al-kubrā* (Cairo: Maktabat Muḥammad al-Malījī, 1315/1897), 2:18–19.

Al-Munāwī said about him, 'An Imam, the crown of his knowledge is raised, his virtue is gathered, the news about his qualities is well known, the pearls of his wisdom are widespread, his written works are beneficial... . He had mastery of the outer sciences and inner gnosis. [He is] an Imam in *tafsīr*, hadith and *uṣūl* [principles of jurisprudence], an ocean in *fiqh*.'[8]

Imam Tāj al-Subkī says about him, 'It appears to me that he was a Shāfi'ī, though others have said that he was a Mālikī, in his school of Islamic law. He was the mentor (*ustādh*) of the shaykh, Imam, my father, in Sufism. He was an authority, a gnostic (*'ārif*), endowed with *ishārāt* and miracles (*karāmāt*) and firmly established in Sufism. He accompanied Shaykh Abū al-'Abbās al-Mursī, the disciple of Shaykh Abū al-Ḥasan al-Shādhilī, and took from him [the spiritual path]. Shaykh Tāj al-Dīn [ibn 'Aṭā' Allāh] settled in Cairo, [where he engaged in] sermonising and guiding people. He has marvellous words, which his students recorded in written form.'[9]

Ḥāfiẓ Ibn Ḥajar said about him, 'He accompanied Shaykh Abū al-'Abbās al-Mursī, the student of al-Shādhilī, and authored [works] on the merits of them both. He was the spokesman for the Sufis of his time, and he is the one who vigorously confronted Shaykh Ibn Taymiyyah, and wrote numerous works in that regard.'[10]

Ḥāfiẓ al-Dhahabi said about him, 'He had an amazing aura and an impact on the hearts and possessed great virtues. He would speak in the grand al-Azhar mosque on a stool with words that revitalised the souls. He would mix the words of the Sufis [literally, the group] with the traditions of the early righteous Muslim community and a vast array of knowledge. Consequently,

8. al-Munāwī, *al-Kawākib al-durriyyah*, 3:8–9.

9. Tāj al-Dīn al-Subkī, *Ṭabaqāt al-Shāfi'iyyah al-kubrā*, 2nd edn. (Cairo: Dār Iḥyā' al-Kutub al-'Arabiyyah, 1383/1964), 9:23.

10. Ibn 'Imād al-Ḥanbalī, *Shadharāt al-dhahab* (Damascus: Dār Ibn Kathīr, 1413/1992), 8:37.

his followers grew in number. He was endowed with clear signs of goodness. Al-Kamāl Ja'far said, "He heard [hadiths] from al-Abraqūhī, and studied grammar with al-Māzūnī, and undertook learning *fiqh* and literature."'[11]

Imam Suyūṭī has said, 'The sermons of Tāj al-Dīn ibn 'Aṭā' Allāh would be attended by the likes of Shaykh Taqī al-Dīn al-Subkī, the Imam of his time in *tafsīr*, hadith, *fiqh*, theology, the principles of jurisprudence and both textually transmitted [*manqūl*] and rational [*ma'qūl*] sciences; [indeed, he was] rather the *mujtahid* after whom there was no one like him nor before him for a long time.'[12]

Imam Ibn 'Aṭā' Allāh passed away in Cairo at the Manṣūriyyah school in the thirteenth century CE in the month of Jumāda al-Ākhirah in 709 AH ﷺ.

11. *Ibid.*

12. 'Abd al-Raḥmān al-Suyūṭī, *Ta'yīd al-ḥaqīqah al-'aliyyah* [Defending the lofty reality], 2nd edn. (Beirut: Dār al-Fātiḥ, 1415/1994), 69.

The Refinement of Souls

Introductory remarks

All praise is due for Allah, the Lord of the Worlds; and may He send down His blessings upon our master Muhammad, his family and all his Companions.

This book, *The Bride's Crown: Comprising the Souls' Refinement*, is the compilation of the Shaykh, the Imam, the one who joined between the knowledge of the Shariah and the *ḥaqīqah*,[1] Tāj al-Dīn Abū al-'Abbās Aḥmad ibn 'Aṭā' Allāh al-Sakandarī. May Allah ﷻ have mercy on him and shelter him in the midst of His garden, and shower his blessings upon us and [all of] the Muslims. May Allah send His blessings and peace upon our master Muhammad and his Companions. *Āmīn*.[2]

---

1. 'Shariah is the [Divine] command for creation to adhere to servitude [to Him in accordance with what He has legislated for them on the tongues of His prophets and messengers], whereas the *ḥaqīqah* [reality] is to behold [with one's heart Allah's] Lordship. Therefore, every Shariah that is not supported by the *ḥaqīqah* is unacceptable, while every *ḥaqīqah* that is not bound by the Shariah is futile. Thus, the Shariah came to obligate mankind with responsibilities, whereas the *ḥaqīqah* came to inform [us] about the Real's disposing [of affairs in creation]; the Shariah is that you worship Him, whilst the *ḥaqīqah* is that you behold Him; the Shariah is to undertake what one has been commanded with, whilst the *ḥaqīqah* is to behold what He has ordained and apportioned (*qaḍā wa qadar*) and what He has concealed and revealed. Ustādh Abū 'Alī al-Daqqāq ؓ said, "Know that Shariah is *ḥaqīqah* in that it has been made compulsory by His command, and *ḥaqīqah* is also Shariah in that gnosis of Him ﷻ has been made compulsory by His command."' Zakariyyā al-Anṣārī, *Sharḥ al-Risālah al-Qushayriyyah* (n.p., 1367/1957), 43.

2. This introductory paragraph is from the scribe, who is most likely one of the author's disciples; as for the author's words, they begin in the following paragraph from 'O slave, petition...'.

Repentance to Allah

O slave, petition Allah to enable you to repent at all times, because Allah has exhorted you to it: 'O believers, all of you are to repent to Allah, so that you may succeed' [Qur'an 24:31]; and He ﷻ said, 'Verily, Allah loves the oft-repentant, and He loves those who purify themselves' [Qur'an 2:222]. Furthermore, the Messenger of Allah ﷺ said, 'Verily, I seek forgiveness from Allah seventy times a day.'

If you want to repent, then let no moment of your life be devoid of reflection. Reflect on what you did during your day: if you find therein an act of obedience, be thankful to Allah for it; and if you find therein an act of disobedience, reproach yourself for that, seek Allah's forgiveness and repent to Him. The most beneficial occasion for you is to sit (*majlis*) before Allah and reproach yourself. Do not reproach yourself while laughing and merry; instead, reproach yourself while serious and genuine, frowning, sad-hearted, broken and abased. If you do this, Allah will transform your condition from one of sadness to joy, humility to honour, darkness to light and from being veiled to [receiving] disclosure [of higher spiritual realities].

It is related that Shaykh Makīn al-Dīn ﷺ,[3] who was from amongst the *Abdāl*,[4] said, 'I used to be a tailor in the beginning of my affair [i.e. the beginning of my spiritual journey to Allah]

3. Shaykh Makīn al-Dīn al-Asmar is: 'Abū 'Abd-Allāh ibn Manṣūr al-Sakandarī al-Shādhilī. He was born and raised in Alexandria, where he memorised the Qur'an and excelled in its sciences. He was considered the shaykh of the various canonical readings (*qirā'āt*) [of the Qur'an] and many great men would come to benefit from him. He was known for spiritual struggle (*mujahādāt*), amazing states and strange unveilings (*mukāshafāt*). He passed away in Alexandria in 692 AH and was buried next to Abū al-'Abbās al-Mursī ﷺ.' Muḥyī al-Dīn al-Ṭu'mā, *al-Ṭabaqāt al-Shādhiliyyah al-kubrā* (Beirut: Dār al-Jīl, 1416/1996), 220.

4. *Abdāl* (plural of *badl*), literally, substitutes, are distinguished saints. Imam Aḥmad has narrated in his *Musnad* with a chain of transmission in which there is weakness, but it nevertheless has support: 'The substitutes

and would feed myself through that means, and I used to count my words during the day. Then, when evening would arrive, I would take myself to account, and I would find my words to be few; so whatever good I found in them, I would praise Allah and thank Him for it; and for the rest, I would repent to Allah and seek His forgiveness.' [Thus, he persisted] until he became one of the *Abdāl* ﷺ.

Know that if you have an agent who holds his self to account and demands from it his rights, then you do not need to take him to account, because he does so himself. However, if he does not do so, then you would have to take him to account and demand your rights from him and do so rigorously. Accordingly, all your works should be for Allah ﷻ; and do not think [for a moment] that you do anything without Allah ﷻ taking you to account and demanding from you His rights.

If a slave commits a sin, darkness accompanies it. Disobedience is like fire, with darkness as its smoke. If someone was to light a fire in his house for seventy years, do you not see that it will become black? Similarly, the heart becomes black by acts of disobedience. Consequently, it is not purified except by repentance to Allah. Humiliation, darkness and being veiled [from Allah] accompany acts of disobedience. If you repent to Allah, the traces of sins will disappear.

Negligence does not encroach on you except as a consequence of your negligence in emulating the Prophet ﷺ. And you will not attain honour in Allah's sight except by emulating him ﷺ.

(*abdāl*) in this nation are thirty men whose hearts are in accordance with the heart of Ibrāhīm, the All-Merciful's friend. Whenever a man [amongst them] passes away, Allah substitutes a man in his place.' Al-Ḥakīm al-Tirmidhī has an addition in his narration from Abū Dardā': 'They did not outstrip people by profusely praying, fasting and invoking the glorification of Allah (*tasbīḥ*), but rather by good character, genuine scrupulousness, good intentions and purity of hearts. Those are Allah's party (*ḥizb Allāh*). Surely, Allah's party are the ones who are successful.'

Types of emulation

Emulation of him ﷺ is of two types: apparent and subtle. The apparent is like prayer, fasting, giving charity, performing pilgrimage, struggling (*jihād*) and so forth. The subtle is that you totally absorb yourself in beholding Allah alone in your prayer, and reflect and ponder on what you recite.

When you perform an act of obedience, like the prayer or recitation [of the Qur'an], but find in it neither complete absorption in Allah nor reflection, then know that you have a hidden disease, such as pride, conceit or the like. Allah ﷻ said, 'I shall avert My signs from those who behave arrogantly on earth without a right' [Qur'an 7:146]. [In such a state,] you are like a person with a fever who finds the taste of sugar to be bitter.

An act of disobedience accompanied by humiliation and impoverishment is better than an act of obedience accompanied by pride and arrogance. Allah ﷻ, relating from Ibrāhīm the Friend [of Allah] (upon him and our Prophet be the best blessings and perfect greetings), said, 'So whoever follows me, then he is with me' [Qur'an 14:36]. Thus, it is understood that whoever does not follow him is not with him. Moreover, Allah ﷻ, relating from Nūḥ (upon him and the Chosen One be the purest of blessings and greetings), said, 'Verily, my son is from my family' [Qur'an 11:45], so He replied, 'He is not from your family;[5] surely, he [has done] an unrighteous deed' [Qur'an 11:46]. Therefore, emulation renders one as if he is a part of the one being emulated, even if one is not related by kinship. Such was the case with Salmān the Persian ؓ, whom the Prophet ﷺ

---

5. 'In other words, he is not from those of your family whom I have promised salvation. This [latter interpretation] is the opinion of Saʿīd ibn Jubayr. However, the majority [of the exegetes] have said, "That is, he is not from the people of your religion nor your guardianship." This proves that the ruling pertaining to sharing the same religion is greater than the ruling pertaining to [a common] lineage.' Abū ʿAbd-Allāh al-Qurṭubī, *Tafsīr al-Qurṭubī*, 2nd edn. (Beirut: Dār Iḥyāʾ al-Turāth al-ʿArabī, 1405/1985), 9:46.

described in the following words, 'Salmān is from us, the People of the Household.' It is well known that Salmān was of Persian origin, but due to his emulation, he [the Prophet ﷺ] described him in such terms so as to teach us. While emulation can establish such bonds, the lack of emulation causes separation.

Where will you find goodness?

Allah has gathered all goodness in a house and made its key the emulation of the Prophet ﷺ. Therefore, emulate him by being content with whatever Allah has given you as provision, and abstaining and reducing your attachment to this world and to what does not concern you in words and deeds. Whoever has the door of emulation opened for him, it is a proof of Allah's love for him. He ﷺ has said, 'Say: "If you love Allah, then follow me; Allah will love you and forgive you your sins. Allah is Oft-Forgiving, Merciful"' [Qur'an 3:31].

If you desire complete goodness, then say, 'O Allah, I ask You to enable me to emulate Your Messenger ﷺ in words and deeds.' Whoever seeks that should not wrong Allah's slaves by maligning them. If people had avoided wronging one another, they would have swiftly reached Allah. However, they were impeded like a heavily indebted person who is being constantly harassed by his creditor [for the settling of a debt].

Know that if you had a privileged status with a king and had an intimate relationship with him, and someone arrived pursuing you because of a debt, then the king would be stern with you, even if the debt were a minuscule amount. So what will you do when you arrive on the Day of Resurrection, when a hundred thousand people or more are after you because of various debts, such as usurping property, sullying their reputation and the like? How will your state be then?

The truly unfortunate person is he whose sins and base desires have obliterated him until they have left him like a worn-out water skin. This is someone who is truly deprived and to whom condolences are offered. His food and appetites have disappeared: he has filled the toilet and pleased his wife with them. If only they were from a lawful [source]!

Repentance gains Allah's love ﷻ

Thus the first station is repentance, and what follows it is not accepted except by virtue of it.

The similitude of a slave when he does an act of disobedience is like that of a new pot: each time it is heated, it increases in blackness. If you hasten to wash it, the blackness will be washed off it, but if you leave it and cook in it, time after time, you will have consolidated the blackness until it disintegrates, and washing it thereafter will be of no use.

Repentance is therefore that which washes the blackness of the heart so that deeds appear with the fragrance of acceptance over them. So ask Allah to enable you to constantly repent. If you achieve it, then your time will be delightful, because it is a gift from Allah that He allots to whomever He wills of His slaves. It may so happen that a slave with cracked heels achieves it, but not his master; or a woman achieves it, but not her husband; or a young man achieves it, but not his elder. Therefore, if you achieve it, then Allah truly loves you, for He ﷻ has said, 'Verily, Allah loves the oft-repentant, and He loves those who purify themselves' [Qur'an 2:222].

Only someone who knows the true, precious value of something will wish for it. If you were to quickly scatter rubies among beasts, [they would pay no attention because] barley would have been more preferable to them. Look therefore at which of the [following] two groups you belong to? If you repent, you are from amongst those beloved [by Allah]; but if you do not, then you are from amongst the transgressors. Allah ﷻ has said, 'And whoever does not repent, then he is from the transgressors' [Qur'an 49:11].

Whoever repents has won, and whoever does not has lost. Do not despair and ask, 'How often do I repent yet violate [my repentance by acts of disobedience];' for a sick person hopes for life as long as the soul remains alive.

When a slave [of Allah] repents, his abode in Paradise rejoices for him, the heavens and the earth rejoice for him, and so does the Messenger ﷺ. The Real ﷻ was not satisfied for you to be a lover; rather, He wants you to be a beloved. And where is the beloved [in status] compared to the lover?

Woe to a slave who knows of the kindness of the Benevolent, yet dares to disobey Him! But the one who preferred to disobey Him did not realise His kindness. The one who was not vigilant of Him did not know His rank. The unfortunate one is he who occupied himself with other than Him and knew that his self (*nafs*)[6] was summoning him towards destruction as he followed it; and knew that his heart was inviting him to guidance

6. The *nafs*, often translated as the lower self, or merely the self, or the ego, has been technically defined by the Sufis like Imam Qushayrī and Shaykh Zakariyyā al-Anṣārī, who have said, '[Qushayrī:] they [the Sufis] only mean by *nafs* that which is blameworthy in [relation to] a slave's qualities and blameworthy in [relation to] his actions and manners. [Anṣārī:] frequently they use it to express that which is the source of blameworthy qualities, because of His words ﷻ "Verily, the self (*nafs*) is ever commanding [one to do] evil", which is why it is considered to be a man's worst enemy, as it is difficult to save oneself from its evil. Do you not see that if a person reconciles with all of his enemies, then he is safe from their evil; but if he wants to reconcile with his lower self, then it will destroy him. This is why struggling against it is the greatest struggle (*al-jihād al-akbar*).' Further on, Shaykh Zakariyyā says, 'The self by its very nature inclines towards this world (*dunyā*) because it does not know of anything other than it as good. But when it realises its deficiency, and its being a barrier between good deeds, it becomes averse to it, until that which was delightful to it becomes detestable to it, even though its nature has not changed; rather what has changed is its perception of what is delightful and what is detestable. Likewise, whoever looks towards righteous actions and the difficulty in undertaking them, he finds his self averse to them; but if he then realises the benefits that result from their performance, he inclines towards them and detests forsaking them...' al-Anṣārī, *Sharḥ al-Risālah al-Qushayriyyah*, 44.

yet he disobeyed it; and knew the rank of the One who was disobeyed yet confronted Him with disobedience (If he knew that grandeur was His attribute, he would not have confronted Him with disobedience.); and knew the proximity of his Master yet rushed towards that which He has prohibited; and knew the consequences of both outer and inner sins in the Hereafter yet lacked modesty before His Lord; and if he knew that he was completely in His grasp, he would not have opposed Him.

Outer and inner effects of acts of disobedience

Know that disobedience consists of breaching the covenant [with Allah] and untying the bond of love, giving preference [to one's lower self] over the Master, obedience to one's whims, the removal of the robe of modesty, and defying Allah by doing that which displeases Him. In addition, there are apparent effects, such as the appearance of turbidity in one's limbs,[7] stiffness in the eyes,[8] lethargy in service [to Allah], negligence in guarding the sacred,[9] the rise in pursuing base desires and the disappearance of the splendour of obedience.

As for the subtle effects, they are things such as the hardness of the heart, stubbornness of the self, constriction of the chest due to [being subservient to] base desires, loss of sweetness in [performing] acts of obedience, continuous distractions [literally, 'others' (*aghyār*), that turn one] from Allah and prevent the radiance of spiritual lights, prevalence of the state of whim, and so forth,

7. This is a figure of speech for the disappearance of the splendour of light from his face and limbs because of his acts of disobedience.

8. This is a figure of speech for the lack of weeping. Weeping is indicative of mercy in one's heart.

9. This negligence is due to the complacency in committing contraventions to the Sacred Law, as one sin leads to another to the point that one no longer reveres the Sacred Law.

such as the succession of doubts, forgetting the final destination and [what will be] the prolongation of accountability [on the Day of Judgement].

If there was nothing in an act of disobedience other than the change in one's name, then that would have been enough [as a deterrent]. In other words, if you are obedient, you will be called devout, whereas if you are disobedient, you will be called a negligent sinner. This is in terms of the change in one's name, so what about the change in effect, such as being transformed from experiencing sweetness in obedience [to Allah] to experiencing sweetness in disobedience [to Allah], and from delight in serving Allah to delight in base desire? This is with respect to change in effect, so what about the change in one's description? After you were described by Allah with beautiful attributes, the matter becomes reversed, so that you are described with blameworthy states and conditions. This is in respect to change in description, so what about the change in rank? So after you were considered righteous in Allah's sight, He now sees you as being from amongst those who sow corruption; and after you were seen by Him as one of the pious, you are now seen by Him as a traitor. So if sins manifest before your face, seek help from Allah and take refuge in Him, throw soil over your head and say, 'O Allah, transport me from the humiliation of disobedience to the honour of obedience.' In addition, [you should] visit the graves of Allah's friends and the righteous and say, "O Most Merciful of the Merciful!"'

The struggle against the lower self

Do you want to struggle against your lower self while empowering it with base desires until they subdue you? If that is the case, then you are ignorant! The heart is a tree that is irrigated by the water of obedience, and its fruits are the states that it experiences: the fruit of the eye is reflection; the fruit of the ears is listening to the

Qur'an; the fruit of the tongue is the remembrance [of Allah]; and the fruit of the hands and feet is striving towards good deeds. If the heart dries up, its fruit will perish.

If the heart is suffering a drought, then profusely invoke Allah. Do not be like a sick person who says, 'I shall not take any medicine until I find a cure,' and so it is said to him, 'You shall not find a cure until you take the medicine.' There is no sweetness in the [spiritual] struggle; there is nothing in it except the heads of spears. So struggle against your self; this is the greatest struggle (*jihād*). Know that a mother who has lost a child has no reason to celebrate. In fact, the only one who has a reason to celebrate is the one who has subdued his self. There is no call for celebration except for the one who has organised his affairs. Someone passed by a monastery and said to the monk, 'O monk, when will these people celebrate?' He replied, 'The day that Allah forgives them.'

The similitude of your behaviour with your self is like that of someone who finds his wife in a pub, and so brings her beautiful clothes and delicious food. Then, when she fails to pray, he begins to feed her sweet pastries and various delicacies.[10]

One of them remained for forty years without attending the congregational prayer because of smelling the foul stench from the hearts of the heedless. How familiar you are with your worldly interests, yet how ignorant you are of your interests in the Hereafter!

Your relation to this world is like that of someone who went out to a fertile land, farmed it and stored away the produce. In other words, you have done something whose benefit you will reap in due course. Yet, if you store away the snakes of desires and the scorpions of disobedience, then you will be destroyed. It is sufficient ignorance on your part that, whilst people store away

10. In other words, instead of deterring it, he begins to assist and encourage it in performing acts of disobedience that it is engaged in.

their staple for when they will need it, you store away that which will actually harm you; namely, acts of disobedience. Have you seen anyone who brings snakes and then nurtures them in his house? Yet here you are, doing exactly that!

The most harmful thing feared for you are sins that you consider trivial, because you are likely to take the enormities seriously and therefore repent from them. But you underestimate the minor sins and so do not repent from them. In this case you are like someone who encounters a lion that Allah saves him from, but is then defeated by fifty wolves. Allah ﷻ has said, 'And you consider it insignificant, though in the sight of Allah it is an enormity' [Qur'an 24:15]. An enormity is insignificant in comparison to Allah's generosity. Nevertheless, if you persist in a minor sin, it becomes an enormity, as poison [eventually] kills in spite of its small doses. A minor sin is like a spark of fire, and a spark may burn down a town.

Whoever spends his well-being and health in disobedience to Allah is like someone whose father has left behind for him a thousand dinars with which he buys snakes and scorpions and puts them around himself; the latter stings him and the other bites him. Will they not kill him? You waste hours in opposition to Him; thus, you are merely like a kite which hovers over a carcass: wherever it finds it, it lands on it. Be like the bee: small in size, but great in its aspiration, as it collects goodness and bears goodness.

How often have you wallowed around in places of tribulation? You are to wallow in that which Allah loves, as this reality will show you your path. But whoever is killed by heedlessness, tragedies will not bring him back to life. Only an unintelligent woman laughs as her son dies. Similarly, you are deprived of standing at night [in prayer] and fasting during the day, and in all of your limbs [is lethargy], yet you do not feel pain! That is only because heedlessness has killed your heart. A living person feels the pain of a needle prick, while the deceased, even if he was slashed to shreds with swords, feels no pain. Therefore, [know that] your heart is dead, so [you must] sit in a gathering of wisdom, because in it there is a fragrant breeze (*nafḥah*) from Paradise, which you find on your way, in your house and in your room. Do not miss such a gathering, even if you are in a state of disobedience. Do not ask about the point of attending the gathering whilst in a state of disobedience which you are unable to forsake. Rather, the archer should shoot; and if he does not hit the target today, then he will do so tomorrow.

Warning against disobedience to Allah

Know that you are to be careful of disobedience, for it may cause sustenance to be suspended.[11] So seek Allah's acceptance of your repentance; and if it is accepted, [then all is well], otherwise seek help from Allah and say, 'O Lord, we have wronged ourselves, and if You do not forgive us, and have mercy on us, we shall surely be of the losers' [Qur'an 7:23]. Do not be like someone who has lived for forty years and has never knocked on Allah's door.

The most terrible fate – may Allah protect us – is feared for you due to the coal of faith being extinguished by the blackness of disobedience! Namely, continually sinning without repentance until the heart turns black.

Be mindful that you do not become lax in your deeds and choose the good things for your toilet! And be careful of your self which is between your two sides, for it is the one endeavouring to destroy you. Moreover, it does not part from a person until death. At least the devil leaves [you alone] during Ramadan, because during it, the devils are shackled;[12] when you find someone killing

---

11. Ibn Ḥibbān narrated in his *Ṣaḥīḥ* on the authority of Thawbān that he said, 'The Messenger of Allah ﷺ said, "A man is deprived of sustenance (*rizq*) due to a sin that he commits..."' Its chain of transmission is authentic.

12. Both al-Bukhārī and Muslim narrated it. The narration of Muslim on the authority of Abū Hurayrah ؓ is that the Messenger of Allah ﷺ said, 'When Ramadan comes, the doors of Paradise are opened, the doors of the Hellfire are closed and the devils are chained.'

and stealing during it, then [know that] this is from the self [and not the devil]. If the self inclines towards disobedience, remind it of Allah's torment and severance from Him as its consequence.

Poisoned honey is left untouched because of the harm it contains, despite one knowing its sweetness. The Prophet ﷺ said, 'The world is sweet and lush,'[13] and he also described it as 'a gross carcass'.[14] It is sweet and lush to those oblivious and a gross carcass to the intelligent; sweet and lush to the lower selves and a gross carcass to the mirrors of the hearts; and sweet and lush as an admonition, and a gross carcass as a means of [causing] repulsion. Therefore, do not be deceived by its sweetness, because its outcome is bitter.

If you are asked, 'Who is a believer?' say, 'The one who is aware of his own flaws and does not ascribe a flaw to anyone else,' and if it is said to you, 'Who is the one who has been forsaken [by Allah]?' say, 'The one who ascribes blemishes to others, yet exonerates himself of them.'

At present, one of the things people persist in is their conviviality and socialising with the disobedient. If only their faces frowned [whilst witnessing disobedience], it would have deterred them from committing acts of disobedience.

If the door to perfection was opened for you, you would not have returned to vice. Tell me, if someone who has the doors of palaces opened for him, will he return to rubbish heaps? Had He opened for you the door to intimacy between yourself and Him, you would not have sought anyone else for intimacy. If He had

---

13. Muslim narrated it on the authority of Abū Sa'īd from the Prophet ﷺ that he said, 'Verily, this world is sweet and lush, and verily Allah has placed you therein as a vicegerent to see how you behave; so guard yourself from this world and guard yourself from women, for the first tribulation of Banī Isrā'īl was because of women.'

14. Abū Nu'aym narrates from Imam 'Alī – may Allah ennoble his face – that he said, 'This world is a carcass, so whoever wants it, then let him be patient in mingling with dogs.'

chosen you for His Lordship, He would not have severed you from Himself. If you had been honourable in His sight, He would not have cast you aside to someone else.

If He removes from you the love of creation, then rejoice, for this is from His concern for you. There is no act of disobedience except it is accompanied by humiliation. Do you disobey Him, thinking He will honour you? Surely not! He has correlated honour with obedience, and humiliation with disobedience. Obedience to Him has become a light and [a source of] honour and an uncovering of the veil [that prevents one from beholding Him]; and its opposite is disobedience, darkness, humiliation and the veil between yourself and Him. But nothing has deprived you from beholding Him other than your trespassing the bounds and occupying yourself with this existence (*wujūd*).

If your child is disobedient, discipline him with the Sacred Law, but do not ostracise him; rather, confront him with a frown so that he may desist from disobedience. A believer is usually vulnerable to deception [from Satan] when he is disobedient [to Allah], for they either disgrace him or mock him.[15] If they do that, they have strayed off the right path. If a believer commits an act of disobedience, he has fallen into a great predicament, and the way to rectify him is to treat him like your disobedient child: you outwardly shun him, whilst inwardly you have mercy on him and privately pray for him.

15. In other words, Satan tricks and deceives him as a consequence of their behaviour towards him. It has been narrated by al-Bukhārī on the authority of Abū Hurayrah that he said, 'A man who had drunk [wine] was brought to the Prophet ﷺ, and so he said [to his Companions], "Strike him."'Abū Hurayrah said, 'Some of us were hitting him with their hands, others hitting him with their shoes and some hitting him with their garments. Then, when he was leaving, someone said, "May Allah disgrace you," whereupon the Prophet said, "Do not say such; do not assist Satan against your brother."' In a variant of Abū Hurayrah's hadith, 'Someone said, "What is the matter with him? May Allah disgrace him!" So the Messenger of Allah ﷺ said, "Do not assist Satan against your brother."'

Envy is sheer ignorance

You are sufficiently ignorant to envy worldly-minded people for what they have been given and occupy your heart with what they have. But you are even more ignorant than them, because they are occupied with what they have been given, while you are occupied with something you have not been given.

Your eye is inflamed, so you treat it, and the only reason for that is that you have experienced the delights of this world. You treat it so that your gaze is not deprived of its delights, while your inner sight suffers inflammation for forty years, yet you do not treat it.

Know that if the beginning of your life has been wasted, then it is fitting that its ending be safeguarded. If a woman had ten children, but nine of them died and one remained, would she not give her total affection to that remaining one? Even though you have wasted most of your life, safeguard what is left of it, which is only a short time. By Allah, your life does not begin from the time you were born; nay, your life begins from the day you knew Allah ﷻ.

What a world of difference there is between felicitous people and wretched people! When felicitous people see a person committing acts of disobedience to Allah, they outwardly condemn him, while privately praying for him. In contrast, wretched people, [upon witnessing such disobedience] may condemn the person for self-gratification and even tarnish his reputation. In fact, a true believer is someone who sincerely advises his brother in private, while concealing his faults in public. In this regard the wretched are the opposite: if they see a person committing an act of disobedience, they shut the door on him and disgrace him because of it. Consequently, the wretched do not have illuminated insights, and they are remote from Allah.

If you wish to test the intelligence of a man, observe him when you mention another person to him. If you notice him looking to find fault in him until he ends up saying to you, 'Spare us of him! That person has done such and such!' then you should know that his internal state is in ruins, and there is no hint of gnosis in him. On the other hand, if you see that he mentions him positively, or when something blameworthy is mentioned about him, he finds a positive explanation for him, and says 'maybe he forgot', or some similar excuse, then know that his inward state is flourishing, for a believer endeavours to protect the honour of his Muslim brother.

Whoever realises the immediacy of his departure hastens to acquire provisions

Whoever approaches the end of his life, and wishes to redress what he has missed out on, should remember [Allah] with comprehensive invocations. If he was to do that, then his short life will become extended. An example of such a comprehensive invocation is:

$$\text{سُـبْحَانَ اللهِ الْعَظِيْمِ وَبِحَـمْدِهِ، عَدَدَ خَلْقِـهِ، وَرِضَـا نَفْسِـهِ ، وَزِنَةَ عَرْشِـهِ، وَمِدَادَ كَلِمَـاتِه}$$

'Glory be to Allah the Almighty together with His praise, by the number of His creation, His good pleasure, the weight of His throne and the ink of His words.'[16]
Subḥān Allāh al-ʿAẓīm wa bi ḥamdihi, ʿadada khalqihi wa riḍā nafsihi wa zinata ʿarshihi wa midāda kalimātihi.

---

16. Muslim (2726) and others have narrated on the authority of Juwayriyah ☙ that the Prophet ﷺ one day left her after the dawn prayer, while she was [sitting] in her place of prayer. He then returned after mid-morning, as she was [still] sitting, and said, 'You are still in the same position as when I left you?' She replied, 'Yes.' The Prophet ﷺ said, 'I said after [I left] you four phrases thrice, that if they were to be weighed against what you have said today, they would outweigh them: "Glory be to Allah the Almighty together with His praise, by the number of His creation, His good pleasure, the weight of His throne and the ink of His words".'

Similarly, if you failed to profusely fast and pray, then you should occupy yourself with invoking blessings upon the Messenger of Allah ﷺ; for if you were to do every act of obedience throughout your life, and Allah were to send down His blessing (*ṣalāt*) upon you once, then that one blessing would outweigh all the acts of obedience that you have done throughout your life. That is because you invoke blessings upon the Prophet ﷺ according to your capacity, whereas He sends down His mercy according to His Lordship. If this is the case with just a single invocation of blessings, then what about when He sends down upon you ten [blessings] for each one [you invoke], as has been related in the authentic tradition? How fine a life it is to obey Allah therein by remembering Him ﷻ or invoking blessings upon Allah's Messenger ﷺ!

It has been related that there is not a game that is caught, nor a tree that is cut, except as a consequence of its heedlessness from the remembrance of Allah ﷻ. A burglar does not burgle a house while its inhabitants are awake; rather, he does so when they are oblivious or asleep.

Whoever knows the immediacy of his departure will hasten in acquiring provisions. Whoever knows that someone else's devotional acts are of no benefit to him, will endeavour to do the same himself [so that he actually benefits]. Whoever spends without counting, will end up bankrupt without realising. Whoever appointed an agent, will dismiss him upon learning of his betrayal. Likewise, you have realised your self's betrayal, so dismiss it and be stern with it.

If you see in yourself apathy [to obedience], base desires, and obliviousness, then [know that] these are attributes from yourself. But if you see in yourself remorse (*inābah*), humility, and abstinence, then these are from the workings of Allah. Similarly, if you see in your country alfa [a water plant], or thorns or boxthorn, then [you know that] this is a plant from your country's earth. Yet, if you see in it moist peony, musk or amber, then you know that it has been brought about by the workings of Allah, because it is not one of the plants that grow in your land, for musk is from Iraqi gazelles and amber is from the Indian Ocean.

The reality of faith

When you disobey Allah ﷻ, your faith is like that of the eclipsed sun or a lamp covered with a plate; in other words, the light [of faith] is blocked due to being covered. You attend the [religious] gathering in the Grand Mosque to enrich your mind; even if your life is short, it is stretched because of faith, humility, subservience, awe [of the Divine], pondering, reflecting and so forth. If you had realised [true] faith, you would not have approached disobedience. There is no debtor more procrastinating than the self,[17] no enemy greater than the devil and no opponent stronger than whim.

Nothing repels the descent of divine succour like pride. Rain only settles on shallow lands, not on mountain peaks. Similarly, mercy falls from the hearts of the arrogant and descends on the hearts of the humble. What is meant by the arrogant are those who rebuff [Allah's] right, not those whose clothes are elegant: 'However, pride is the denunciation of [Allah's] right and contempt for people.'[18] Do not think that pride is only found in a vizier or an affluent person; on the contrary, it may be found in someone who does not have supper for the night, yet he sows

---

17. This is because the self delays one from repenting and desisting from committing sins.

18. Muslim (91) and others have narrated on the authority of ʿAbd-Allāh ibn Masʿūd ﷺ that he said, 'The Messenger of Allah ﷺ said, "No one with an atom's weight of pride in his heart will enter Paradise." So a man said, "A man loves his clothes to be elegant and his shoes to be elegant?" He replied, "Verily, Allah is beautiful and loves beauty. Pride [however] is the denunciation of [Allah's] right and contempt for people."'

corruption and does not rectify [matters], because he disdained Allah Most High's right.[19]

Do not think that the unfortunate person is someone who is a war captive or a prisoner. On the contrary, the truly unfortunate person is someone who disobeys Allah and brings into this pure kingdom the filth of disobedience.

There are many who spend dinars and dirhams, while those who spend tears[20] are few.

The real fool is he who, when his son dies, begins to cry over him yet does not cry over what he has been deprived of by Allah ﷻ. It is as if his state is saying, 'I am crying over what used to busy me from my Lord.' He should, instead, rejoice at that and devote himself to his Master, since He has taken from him that which used to preoccupy him from Him. It is disgraceful that your hair turns white, yet you are still [like] a child in [your lack of] intelligence and do not understand what Allah wants from you! If you are intelligent, cry over yourself before you are cried over. Your child, wife, servant and friend do not cry over you when you die; rather, they cry over what they have missed out on from you. So beat them to the crying and say, 'I deserve to cry over the loss of my portion from my Lord before you cry over me.'

How ignorant you are! Your Master treats you faithfully, while you treat Him callously.

Who is a real man?

A real man is not someone who screams amongst people in gatherings; rather, a real man is only he who screams over his self and steers it back to Allah.

---

19. The printed edition has 'over Allah's creation (*khalq*)', while the manuscript has 'over Allah's right (*ḥaqq*)', which is probably the correct version because he previously mentioned, 'However, pride is denunciation of [Allah's] right.'

20. In another edition it reads 'souls' instead of 'tears'.

Whoever is concerned with this world and not bothered about the Hereafter is like someone to whom a lion approaches for the kill, and then a flea comes and bites him, and so he becomes distracted with the flea from paying any attention to the lion. Whoever is heedless of Allah busies himself with the trivial, whereas the one who is not heedless of Him will preoccupy himself with none other than Him. The best state for you is to lose this world in order to gain the Hereafter. How often you have lost the Hereafter to gain this world! How awful is fear in a soldier! How awful is a grammatical error from a grammarian! How awful is the pursuit of this world for someone who feigns abstinence from it!

A true man is not someone who nurtures you through his words; rather, a true man is only he who nurtures you through his gaze.

The blessing of the gaze from a friend of Allah (walī)

It has been related that Shaykh Abū al-ʿAbbās al-Mursī ﷺ[21] said, 'If a tortoise nurtures its hatch with its gaze, then likewise a shaykh nurtures his disciples with his gaze; for a tortoise hatches its eggs on land, heads towards the river, and gazes at its hatch; then Allah nurtures them through its gaze upon them.'

Beware lest you leave this abode while not having tasted the sweetness of His love. The sweetness of His love is not in food and drink, as even disbelievers and beasts have that in

21. He is Aḥmad Abū al-ʿAbbās al-Mursī. He was amongst the greatest gnostics, and it has been said that he was the only inheritor of Shaykh Abū al-Ḥasan al-Shādhilī's knowledge ﷺ. He is the foremost of those who took the spiritual path from the latter. He would say, 'The knowledge of this group [Sufis] is the knowledge of realisation, and the knowledge of realisation cannot be carried by the intellects of the majority of creation.' Similarly, his shaykh, Abū al-Ḥasan al-Shādhilī, would say, 'My books are my disciples.' He passed away in 686 AH. al-Shaʿrānī, *al-Ṭabaqāt al-kubrā* (Cairo: Maktabat Muḥammad al-Malījī, 1315/1897), 2:11.

common with you. Instead, join the angels in the sweetness of His remembrance and utter devotion to Allah ﷻ, because the souls cannot bear the dribble of the egos. If they are immersed in the carcass of this world, then they will not be fit to attain presence of the heart [with Allah], because Allah's proximity ﷻ (*hadrah*)[22] is not accessible to those defiled by the impurity of disobedience. So purify your heart from blemishes, and the door to the unseen shall open up for you. Furthermore, repent to Allah and return to Him with penitence and remembrance. Whoever continues to knock on the door, it shall be opened for him. If it was not for civility, we would have said to you what has been mentioned by Rābi'ah 'Adawiyyah ﵉,[23] 'When has this door been closed for it to be opened?' This is a door that will deliver you unto His proximity.

Beware of the heart's obliviousness of Allah's Oneness (*waḥdāniyyah*), since the first stage of those who occupy themselves with the remembrance of Allah is to be mindful of His Oneness ﷻ. Those who [truly] remember Him only remember Him, and things are only disclosed to them by virtue of this constant recollection; and they were not expelled [from spiritual witnessing] except due to their remembrance that was dominated by heedlessness. You can seek assistance in overcoming that [heedlessness] by suppressing the two desires: the stomach and the genitals.[24] Nothing stands between you and Allah except your lower self.

---

22. 'Know that what is meant by Allah's proximity (*hadrah*) ﷻ whenever uttered on the tongues of the group [of Sufis] is the servant's beholding (*shuhūd*) himself as being before Allah ﷻ; as long as this is what he beholds, then he is in Allah's proximity.' 'Abd al-Majīd al-Shurnūbī, *Sharḥ al-Ḥikam*, 8th edn. (Damascus: Dār Ibn Kathīr, 1422/2002), 99.

23. She is also known as Rābi'ah al-Baṣriyyah. She was renowned for her extreme piety and celibacy. She passed away in Basra and was buried there in 180 AH.

24. Al-Bukhāri (6109) and others have narrated on the authority of Sa'd ibn Sa'd ؓ that the Messenger of Allah ﷺ said, 'Whoever guarantees me [that he will guard] what is between his two jawbones and what is between his two legs, I shall guarantee him Paradise.'

Gaining favour with Allah ﷻ

How often you try to gain favour with the creation, yet how seldom you try to gain favour with the Real! If the door to gaining favour with Allah was opened for you, you would see wonders. Two cycles of prayer in the middle of the night, visiting the sick, your praying over the dead, giving charity to the poor, assisting your Muslim brother and the removal of anything harmful from the path are all means of gaining favour [with Allah]. However, the fallen sword requires a forearm [to lift it]. There is no act of worship more beneficial for you than invoking Allah, because it is feasible for an old man and for a sick person who is unable to stand, bow and prostrate.

Know that the scholars and the sages acquaint you with how to present yourself before Allah ﷻ. Have you ever seen a slave who is fit to serve [his master] immediately upon being purchased? On the contrary, he is given to someone who trains and disciplines him, whereupon becoming worthy and learned in the proper etiquette he is presented before the king. Similarly, the disciples of Allah's friends, may Allah be pleased with them, accompany them until they gently nudge them to His presence. In this regard, they are like a swimmer teaching a child how to swim: initially, he accompanies the child until the latter is able to swim by himself; and when he is accomplished, he is pushed out to sea and left to it.

The prophets عليهم السلام *and Allah's friends* رضي الله عنهم *are the greatest means to Him* ﷻ

Beware lest you believe that the prophets, the friends of Allah and the righteous are of no benefit,[25] for surely Allah has made them a means (*wasīlah*) to Him. That is because every miracle of a friend of Allah is a testimony to the veracity of the Prophet ﷺ,

25. In another edition it reads 'Beware, lest you believe the prophets ... are not a means for gaining proximity (*tawassul*) [to Allah]'.

since they only happen to occur at the hands of Allah's friends. These [miracles] include supernatural phenomena, walking on water, flying in the air, disclosure of the unseen, and water springing forth. They were only granted such miracles as a consequence of [their emulation of] the prophets.

It has been related that Shaykh Abū al-Ḥasan al-Shādhilī ؓ[26] said, 'Measure and weigh your self with the prayer; if it [the self] desists from its desires, know that you are felicitous.' Allah ﷻ says, 'Verily, prayer deters [one] from committing obscene and abominable deeds' [Qur'an 29:45]. If you have to drag your feet to the prayer, then cry over yourself. Have you ever seen a lover who does not wish to meet his beloved? Whoever wants to know what his reality is with Allah, and see his standing with Him, then let him look at his prayer: it is either with calmness and humility, or with heedlessness and haste. If you pray without the former two qualities, then throw soil over your head [in disgrace]. Whoever sits with a perfume seller, its fragrance lingers on him. The prayer is the occasion when you sit with Allah ﷻ. So if you

---

26. He is 'Alī ibn 'Abd-Allāh ibn 'Abd al-Jabbār al-Shādhilī, from Shādhilah, a village in North Africa; the blind ascetic who settled in Alexandria and became the Shaykh of the Shādhilī Order. He was highly esteemed and lofty, and had many Sufi utterances (*'ibārāt*) and allegories (*rumūz*). He accompanied Shaykh Najm al-Dīn Iṣfahānī, Ibn Mashīsh and others. He frequently performed the pilgrimage, and in one of the years, as he was in the 'Aydhāb desert on his way to pilgrimage, he passed away and so was buried there; this was in the month of Dhū al-Qa'dah in 656 AH. Abū 'Abd-Allāh ibn al-Nu'mān attested to his reaching the rank of Quṭb, who brought to this path wonders upon wonders. Shaykh Ibn Daqīq al-'Īd would say about him, 'I have not seen anyone with a deeper gnosis than Shaykh Abū al-Ḥasan ؓ.' He [Shaykh Abū al-Ḥasan] used to say, 'If your spiritual unveiling (*kashf*) contradicts the Book and the Sunnah, then adhere to the Book and the Sunnah and leave the spiritual unveiling, and say to yourself, "Indeed, Allah has guaranteed immunity (*'iṣmah*) for me in the Book and the Sunnah, but did not guarantee it for me in [my] spiritual unveiling, nor [in my] inspiration (*ilhām*), nor [in my] beholding (*mushāhadah*) [of higher spiritual realities]."' al-Sha'rānī, *al-Ṭabaqāt al-kubrā*, 2:4.

sit with Him, yet you do not gain anything from Him, then that indicates a disease in your heart, such as pride, conceit, or poor etiquette. Allah ﷻ said, 'I shall avert My signs from those who display arrogance on the earth without a right' [Qur'an 7:146]. Therefore, whoever has performed the prayer, he should not leave hastily. Instead, he should remember Allah ﷻ and seek His forgiveness due to his shortcomings therein, since many a prayer is not worthy of acceptance. If you seek Allah's forgiveness after its performance, it will be accepted. When the Prophet ﷺ would pray, he would seek Allah's forgiveness three times [after the prayer].

How many states are hidden in you! When trials and tribulations befall, they are revealed. The most sinful of them is doubt about Allah; and doubt about one's provisions is in reality a doubt about the Provider [Himself].

The triviality of this world (dunyā)

This world is too trivial for one to be occupied with it. Due to aspirations becoming trivial, people have become occupied with the trivial. If you were significant, then you would be occupied with what is significant. Whoever occupies himself with the trivial and leaves that which is important, we regard him to be a fool.

Undertake the duties and tasks of servitude that are required of you, and He shall undertake that which He has committed Himself to. Does He provide for insects, while forgetting to provide for you? Allah ﷻ said, 'And enjoin prayer on your people, and steadfastly persevere in doing so. We do not ask you for any provisions; We are the ones who provide for you. The [good] end belongs to the righteous' [Qur'an 20:132].

Whoever is mindful of Allah's right ﷻ, Allah will not create anything in His kingdom except He will inform him thereof. One of them looked at a group of people and said to them,

'Is there anyone amongst you whom Allah informs whenever He creates something in His kingdom?' They replied, 'No.' He said, 'Weep over yourselves.'

The early Muslim community would ask a person about his condition in order to induce him to express gratitude; people today however should not be asked; because if you ask, you will incite them to complain.

It has been related about a grave robber that he repented to Allah ﷻ. One day he said to his shaykh, 'O my master, I have robbed a thousand graves, and have found their faces turned away from the Qiblah!' The shaykh replied, 'My child, that is because of their doubts concerning [their] provision.'

O slave of Allah, if you are to ask Allah [for something], then ask Him to better you in all respects, and that He betters you so that you become content with Him planning your affairs for you.

Moreover, you are a fugitive slave. He asked you to cross over to Him, but [instead] you fled from Him; since fleeing manifests through deeds, states and aspirations. Hence, if you are unmindful in your prayer, speaking gibberish during your fast, or complaining about Allah's kindness, are you not then a fugitive?

Holding one's self to account

It has been related that Shaykh Abū al-Ḥasan al-Shādhilī ﵀ said, 'I once stayed in the desert for three days without anything being unveiled to me. Some Christians passed by and saw me reclining and said, "This is a Muslim priest." They then placed beside my head some food and departed. I said, "How strange! How I have been given provision at the hands of the enemies and not given provision at the hands of loved ones!" Thereupon, it was said [by a hidden voice], "A true man is not someone who is sustained at the hands of his loved ones; rather, a true man is only he who is sustained at the hands of his enemies."'

O you, treat your self like your beast: whenever it strays from the path, hit it, so that it returns to the path. If only you were to treat your self like your coat: whenever it gets dirty, you wash it, and whenever anything of it rips, you mend and fix it; then you would be felicitous. Many a man, his beard having become white, has not sat with Allah for a moment in which he took himself to account. Shaykh Makīn al-Dīn al-Asmar ﷺ used to say, 'In the beginning, I used to take myself to account in the evening and say, "I have said today such and such." So I would find three or four words.' One day, there was with him a shaykh who was around ninety years of age. He [Shaykh Makīn] said, 'O my master, I complain to you of the immensity of [my] sins.' The shaykh replied to him, 'This is something with which we are not familiar; I am not aware of ever committing a sin.'[27]

Just as this world has people who suffice those who depend upon them, the Hereafter also has people who relieve the needs of those who depend upon them. Do not say, 'We have searched but did not find.' If you had searched with sincerity, then you would have found [them]. The reason for you not finding them [i.e. the people of the Hereafter] is your lack of preparation. A bride is not presented before a profligate. If you want to see the bride, then you have to forsake immorality. If you forsake immorality, you will see Allah's friends. Allah's friends are many, and their number does not diminish.[28] If they were to diminish by even one, the light of prophethood would diminish.

---

27. The manuscript copy reads 'And I do not know of ever not committing a sin'.

28. In another edition it reads 'their number does not diminish and nor does their succour'.

If you love someone, you will not reach him until you are worthy of reaching him, and that is not until you have mended your ways. Shaykh Abū al-Ḥasan al-Shādhilī ﵁ said, 'The friends of Allah are like brides, and brides are not seen by criminals.'

The sweetness of faith

If you find acts of obedience and worship burdensome and do not find any sweetness in your heart for them, while acts of disobedience are effortless for you and you find in them sweetness, then know that you are not genuine in your repentance. If the root is healthy, then the fruit will [also] be healthy.

If only you obeyed your Master as your slave obeys you. In other words, you always want your slave to be ready to serve you, and you love to be obeyed. Yet, you seek release from [obedience to] Him as quickly as possible, as if you are pecking with the beak [as you perform the prayer in haste]. If only the sight by which you look at the beauty of others was substituted for blindness.

How much humiliation you have suffered by standing at the doors of creation! And how much have they humiliated you, yet you still do not return to your Master!

It has been related that Shaykh Makīn al-Dīn al-Asmar ﵁ said, 'In a dream I saw a maiden from Paradise saying, "I am for you, and you are for me." Because of her enchanting speech, for two or three months, I was unable to listen to any human speech without vomiting.'

It is enough shunning [of reality] on your part that you open your eyes [in longing] to this abode. Allah ﷻ said, 'And do not stretch your eyes after that with which We have provided different classes of them, (of) the splendour of this world's life, that We may thereby try them' [Qur'an 20:131].

He has ordained for you health and sickness, affluence and poverty, happiness and sadness, so that you may come to know Him by His attributes.

Whoever accompanies you for a day or two and sees no benefit in [accompanying] you, will leave you and accompany someone else; you, on the other hand, accompany your self for forty years, yet you do not see any benefit from it! So say to it, 'Return to the pleasure of your Lord! How often have I conformed to your desires, so turn from idleness to occupation with Allah, from speech to silence, from standing at the doors to sitting in isolation, from intimacy with creation to intimacy with the Creator, and from accompanying the profligate to accompanying the virtuous and pious.'

Turn your states to the opposite of what they used to be: instead of staying awake at night in disobedience to Allah, stay awake at night in obedience to Allah; after inclining towards worldly-minded people, turn away from them and be devoted to Allah; after listening to their speech, lend an ear and listen to the speech and remembrance of Allah ﷻ; and after eating out of greed and desire, eat only a little which assists you to obey [Allah].

Allah ﷻ said, 'Those who strive for Our sake, We shall surely guide them to Our paths' [Qur'an 29:69]. Only someone who is unaware of Allah's punishment will disobey Him; and only someone who is unaware of Allah's reward will fail to obey Him. If they were aware of Allah's punishment, they would not have been oblivious; and if they were aware of what Allah has prepared for the denizens of Paradise, they would not have left it [i.e. obedience to Him] for a blink of an eye.

If you accompany those engrossed with this world, they shall attract you towards it. Yet, if you accompany those engrossed with the Hereafter, they shall attract you towards Allah. The Messenger of Allah ﷺ said, 'A person is in accordance with the religion of his intimate friend, so each one of you should look at whom he takes as an intimate friend.' Just as you select for yourself delicacies in which there is nothing harmful, and a beautiful wife to marry, then likewise do not befriend other than the one who will acquaint you with the path to Allah ﷻ.

A person's close companions

Know that you have three close companions:

1. wealth, which you lose when you die;
2. family, who will leave you behind at the grave;
3. and your works; and they never part from you!

Begin by accompanying the one who shall enter with you in your grave and with whom you will enjoy intimacy;[29] for an intelligent person is one who comprehends Allah's commandments and prohibitions.

Your similitude is like that of a beetle: it lives in dung and excrement, and when a rose is brought close to it, it dies from its fragrance. So too there are amongst people those who are like beetles in their aspirations and like moths in intelligence. A moth continues to throw itself into the fire until it burns therein, so likewise you deliberately throw yourself in the fire of disobedience. If you wanted to journey to Allah, you would have tied your belt. So where is the aspiration?

You only eat to live and not live to eat. If you do the latter, then you are like those things that are found abundantly in places where worms reside. Furthermore, [if you are as such,] then the likes of you are found abundantly amongst beasts. [You should know that] the fastest horse is the lean one. You say, 'Tonight I shall reduce my food intake.' Then, when food is presented before you, it is as if it is a long-lost loved one. For whomsoever Allah does not will his betterment, then words are fatigued in [trying to convince] him. Allah ﷻ said, 'For whomsoever Allah

29. Al-Bukhārī (6149), Muslim (2960) and others have narrated on the authority of Anas ibn Mālik ﷺ that the Messenger of Allah ﷺ said, 'Three things follow the deceased (two of which return, and one remains with him): his family, wealth and deeds. His family and wealth return, while his deeds remain with him.'

wills that he be tried, then you shall not possess anything for him against Allah' [Qur'an 5:41].

How desperately you flee from humiliation, yet how entrenched you are in it! You humiliate your self and throw it into disastrous situations.

One of them said, 'Be with Allah like a child is with his mother: whenever his mother pushes him away [because of the child's own bad behaviour], he throws himself all over her, because he knows that there is no one else to turn to.'

Is there any buyer for our merchandise?

O slave of Allah, you are selective in choosing your delicacies. In fact, you are even selective in choosing the fodder for your riding beast. Yet, you treat Allah arbitrarily! Sometimes you turn over twenty watermelons until you find the one you desire, but that is merely fit for your toilet. You sit cross-legged when eating so that you may expand your intake. Yet, when you come to perform the prayer, you peck like a cockerel, with whisperings and bad thoughts going through your mind as you pray. The similitude of someone whose state is such is like that of someone who sets himself as a target and sits as spears and arrows are shot at him from every angle and direction; is this person not stupid?

The similitude of you listening to wisdom but not acting accordingly is only like that of someone who wears armour but does not fight. Indeed, our merchandise has been advertised, so is there a buyer [out there]?

Your value is of that with which you are occupied. Thus, if you are occupied with this world, then you have no value, because this world is like a worthless carcass.

The best thing that a slave can ask from Allah is that He makes him unwavering [in his relationship] with Him. Allah ﷻ said, 'Keep us guided steadfast on the straight path' [Qur'an 1:5]. So seek guidance and steadfastness from Him, which is for you to be with Allah under all circumstances in [a state] which He is pleased for you, and that is [conforming with] what the Prophet ﷺ conveyed from Allah ﷻ.

Whoever expends pure love for Allah, Allah will make him drink from His pure generosity.

The similitude of the spiritual wayfarer is like that of someone who digs for water little by little until he discovers water after much fatigue. The similitude of the *majdhūb*[30] is like that of someone who sought water and a cloud brought rain for him to take from it without fatigue.

If you give your self every appetite that it desires and seeks, then you are like someone in whose house is a snake that he fattens every day until it ends up killing him. If Allah placed in you a spirit without a self, then you would have obeyed and never disobeyed. In contrast, if He had placed in you a self without a spirit, then you would have disobeyed and never obeyed. Consequently, you waver. He has placed within you a heart, a spirit, a self, and caprice, like a bee in which he has placed the sting and honey: the honey is by virtue of His benevolence (*bi birrihi*),[31] while the sting is by virtue of His overwhelming force (*qahr*). Allah wanted to break the claim of the self by the presence of the heart, and the claim of the heart by the presence of the self.

O slave of Allah, He asked you to be His slave, but you refused except to be the opposite. Your devotion to Allah is your worshipping Him solely and exclusively, so how can He be expected to be pleased with you worshipping other than Him? If you had turned

30. 'A *majdhūb* is someone whom Allah ﷻ is pleased with for Himself and has chosen for His intimate proximity and purified with the water of His sanctity, so he attained the honour and gifts of spiritual stations and degrees without effort and fatigue.' 'Abd al-Mun'im al-Ḥafnī, *al-Mu'jam al-Ṣūfī*, 2nd edn. (Beirut: Dār al-Masīrah, 1407/1987), 236.

31. In the manuscript it reads 'by virtue of His secret (*bi sirrihi*)'.

to Us merely seeking gifts, you would not have done Us justice, so what about[32] when you devote yourself to other than Us?

This world has barred the way to the next, so it impeded the arrival to it; and the Hereafter has stood in the way of the Real, so it prevented the arrival to Him.

Indeed, from Allah's kindness to you is that He discloses to you the flaws and blemishes of yourself, while concealing them from people.

If you are given this world and deprived of gratitude for it, then it is a tribulation for you. The Messenger of Allah ﷺ said, 'A little of this world distracts one from the path to the Hereafter.'

One of them had a wife who said to him, 'I cannot bear for you to be away from me, nor for you to be busy with someone else.' A voice was then heard saying, 'If this is not a creator, nor an originator, yet she loves for your heart to be solely engrossed with her, then how can I not be expected to love for your heart to be solely devoted to Me?'

I once said to Shaykh Abū al-'Abbās al-Mursī ؓ, 'There are things in my self.'[33] The shaykh replied, 'If the self is yours, then do whatever you want with it, though you will not be able to do so.' Then he said, 'The self is like a woman: the more you quarrel with her, the more she quarrels back, so hand it over to its Lord that He may do with it what He wills.' Sometimes you tire yourself out in nurturing it, yet it does not submit to you. A Muslim is therefore someone who hands over his self to Allah, due to the proof in His words ﷻ, 'Indeed, Allah has bought from the believers their persons and wealth in return for Paradise' [Qur'an 9:111].

If your Master loves you, He turns your friends away from you, so that you no longer preoccupy yourself with them, and severs your ties with creation so that you return to Him.

32. In another edition it reads 'so how can He be pleased'.

33. [SM] In other words, there are attachments that trouble it and disturb its moments of pure intimacy with Allah ﷻ.

How often you demand from your self to obey [Allah], yet it slackens! You only need to treat your self in the beginning, and then, when it tastes [Allah's] grace, it will come willingly. Then, the sweetness that you used to experience in disobedience, you shall in turn find it in obedience.

The similitude of faith in the heart is like that of a green tree: when acts of disobedience become too much for it to bear, it dries up and its [ability to] support and benefit dissipates. Whoever wants to fulfil his obligations, then let him forsake the unlawful. Whoever forsakes the offensive (*makrūhāt*) will be assisted in performing good deeds. Whoever forsakes the permissible (*mubāḥ*), He will give him generously beyond imagination and allow him [to enter] His presence. In addition, whoever forsakes listening to whatever is unlawful for him, He shall allow him to truly listen to His speech.[34]

How easy it is for you to do an act of devotion wherein lies caprice for yourself, and how arduous is that in which there is no caprice! An example of this would be if you intended to perform a voluntary hajj but someone suggested that you instead give in charity the amount [you would have spent on the hajj]. In this case, you will find it burdensome; that is because the act of pilgrimage is something seen, so the self finds gratification in it, whereas charity is hidden and forgotten.

A similar situation arises with your studying sacred knowledge when, in reality, it is for other than Allah. For instance, you study throughout the night, whilst you take pleasure in that. Yet, if you are told to pray two cycles at night, you find it burdensome. Again, this is because the two cycles of prayer are solely for Allah ﷻ, without any gratification for the self, whilst the self finds gratification in reading and studying due to participating with others. As a result, it is easy for the self.

One of them said, 'My self craved for marriage, whereupon I saw the *miḥrāb* split open and a shoe made of gold adorned

34. In another edition it reads 'his speech is reduced'.

with pearls emerged.' So it was said to me, "[If] this is her shoe, then what about her face?" Thereafter, the craving for marriage vacated my heart.'

Whoever has lodgings prepared for him will not be satisfied with sitting in rubbish heaps. So perform righteous deeds privately, [keeping them] between yourself and Allah, and do not let your family notice them. Store them away with Allah, so that you will find them on the Day of Resurrection. [This privacy is necessary] because the self takes pleasure in mentioning its deeds. One of them fasted for forty years without his family noticing it.

Do not expend your breaths in other than obedience to Allah. And do not look at the minuteness of the breaths; rather, look at their worth and the reward that Allah will give the slave for [using] them [correctly]. The breaths are jewels! Have you seen anyone throw a jewel in the bin?

Do you improve your exterior yet ruin your interior? [If you only improve your exterior,] then you are like a leper who wears new clothes while puss and serum oozes out of his interior. You rectify that which people witness, yet you do not rectify your heart which is for your Lord!

Wisdom is the chain of a believer

Wisdom is like a chain: if you chain your self to it, it will be restrained; but if you throw it off, it will run loose, and you will be feared for. The similitude of that is like a madman in your house: he ravages it and tears up the clothes; if you chain him, you will be relieved of him; but if you throw off the chain and leave [the house], then the harm will continue.

O old man (*shaykh*), you have wasted your life, so redress what you have missed. You have worn white, which is your white hair; and whiteness should not bear dirt.[35]

---

35. In other words, someone whose hair has turned white should not defile himself with acts of disobedience.

The heart is like a mirror, and the self is like a breath: every time you breathe on the mirror, it is clouded.

The heart of a profligate[36] is like the mirror of a decrepit old woman whose aspiration has grown too weak to polish and look in to it. In contrast, the heart of the gnostic is like the mirror of a bride: she looks in it every day, and so it remains polished.

How to cleanse your heart

The aspiration of those who renounce [this world] is to profusely do good deeds, while the aspiration of the gnostics is to correct their states [with Allah].

There are four things that will help you in cleansing your heart: frequent remembrance [of Allah], constant silence, seclusion, and eating and drinking little.

When those who are oblivious wake in the morning, they examine their wealth; those who renounce this world and worship Allah examine their states; and those who have gnosis of Allah examine their hearts' [attachment] to Allah ﷻ.

There is not a breath that Allah ﷻ brings forth from you, be it an act of worship, an illness or poverty, except that He wants to thereby test you. Whoever seeks this world by means of the Hereafter is like someone who takes a spoon made of ruby to scoop excrement. How could this person not be regarded a fool?

Do not think that people have been merely deprived of knowledge; more than that, they have rather been deprived of divine enablement to obey Him (*tawfīq*).

The first thing that you should cry over is your [lack of] intelligence; just as droughts occur in pastures, so too they occur in the minds of men.

36. In another edition it reads 'the heart of the helpless'.

The greatest blessing

It is by virtue of the intellect that people have lived with one another and with Allah ﷻ: with people through good character, and with Allah by observing those things which please Him.

If Allah favours you with three things, then He has favoured you with the greatest blessing:

1. not trespassing His limits;
2. fulfilling His covenants;
3. and drowning in His presence.

The only reason for your amazement at the states of the gnostics is your immersion in severance [from Allah]. If you had joined them in their travels, you would have joined them in their accounts; and if you had joined them in their difficulties [of their spiritual struggle], then you would have joined them in their bliss.[37]

When you are self-satisfied you are like a tied camel: if you untie it, it will run away. The Messenger of Allah ﷺ said, 'Indeed, the heart of Ādam's son revolves more than [what is in] a boiling pot on the fire.'

How many a person was absorbed in Allah (*jam'*) and then separation came in one moment! Moreover, how many a person spent the night in obedience to Allah and then the sun did not rise until he had severed his relationship with Allah! The heart is similar to the eye: not everything is seen by it; rather, [sight is] only by the extent of the pupil. The heart is similar [to the eye in this respect]. The fleshy organ is not what is meant [by the term heart], but rather the subtlety that Allah has endowed man with; and it is that which is cognisant [of matters]. Allah has made the

37. In the manuscript it reads '*al-fanā*'', which is beholding Allah alone, such that creation disappears from sight.

heart hang from the left side like a bucket, such that if a whim of base desire blows on it, it moves it, and [likewise] if a pious thought blows on it, it is moved by it. So sometimes a whimsical thought prevails over it, and at other times a pious thought prevails over it. This is so that He may occasionally acquaint you with His benevolence and, at other times, familiarise you with His overwhelming force. He makes pious thoughts prevail over the heart when He wants to praise you; and, at other times, He makes whimsical thoughts prevail over it so that He may reproach you. The heart is similar to a ceiling: if a fire is lit in a house, its fumes will rise to the ceiling and blacken it. This is also the case with the smoke of base desire: if it develops in the body, its smoke will rise to the heart and blacken it.

If a misguided person (*ghawī*) wrongs you, return to the Omnipotent (*Qawī*), and do not fear him so that he may overpower you.

Part of faith is to witness everything as coming from Allah ﷻ

The similitude of someone who witnesses harm as coming from the creation is like that of someone who strikes a dog with a stone, and so the dog turns towards the stone to bite it, not realising that the stone is not the doer. In this case, such a person and the dog are the same.

The similitude of someone who witnesses kindness [as coming] from creation is like that of a beast: when it sees its trainer, it waggles its tail [in happiness], yet when its master approaches, it pays no attention to him. If you are intelligent, then witness things as coming from Allah ﷻ, and from no one else.

The one who is truly astray is not someone lost in a jungle, but rather he who has strayed from the path of guidance.

You seek honour from people but not from Allah. Whoever seeks honour from people has strayed off the right track; and whoever strays off the track, his journey only increases his remoteness; this is the one who is truly lost.

If you say, 'There is no deity except Allah,' then Allah will demand it and its right from you, which is that you do not ascribe anything except to Him.

The similitude of the heart if you hand it over to your self is like that of someone who clings on to someone drowning: both of them drown. The similitude of the self if you hand it over to the heart is like that of someone who hands himself over to a proficient swimmer who rescues him. So do not be like the one who hands his heart over to his self. Have you seen a person with sight who hangs onto a blind man to guide him?

If you are able to wake up in the morning and go to sleep at night without having wronged any slave [of Allah], then you are felicitous. And if you do not wrong yourself in that which is between you and Allah, then felicity is perfected for you. So close your eyes, block your ears and beware of wronging Allah's slaves!

Limited intellects

The similitude of you in your lack of intelligence, and not knowing what clothes you are wearing, is only like that of a baby whose mother dresses him with the best and finest clothes without him being aware. He may stain and defile them, so his mother hastens to him and dresses him again so that people do not see him in that [degraded] state. She washes his dirty clothes, while he is unaware of what is happening because of his lack of intelligence.

It has been related that Shaykh Abū al-Ḥasan al-Shādhilī ﷺ said, 'It was said to me, "O 'Alī, clean your clothes of impurities, and you shall get help from Allah in every breath."[38] So I asked,

38. In another edition it reads 'you shall be guarded (*tuḥfaẓ*) by the help of Allah'.

"And what are my clothes?" The reply came, "Allah has dressed you with the garment of gnosis, followed by the garment of Divine Oneness, followed by the garment of love, followed by the garment of faith, and then [finally] the garment of Islam. Whoever knows Allah, everything else becomes insignificant to him. Whoever loves Allah, everything else is trivial to him. Whoever believes Allah to be One does not associate anything with Him. Whoever believes in Allah is safe from everything. Whoever submits himself to Allah will rarely disobey Him; and if he does disobey Him, he apologises to Him; and if he apologises to Him, his apology is accepted."' He said, 'Then I understood the words of the Most High, "And your garments, purify [them]" [Qur'an 74:4].'

O one who has lived yet not lived, you leave this world without having experienced the most delightful thing therein: that is, intimate discourse with the Real ﷻ, and His addressing you. You are cast [on your bed] like a corpse at night. If you are dragged away from Him, then seek help from Allah, and say, 'O angels of Allah, O messenger of my Lord, I have been deprived of the booty which they have attained of the delight in intimate discourse [with Allah] and pure love.'

If a slave is pretentious about his acts of obedience, arrogant towards His creation, puffed up with pride, demanding from others that they give him his rights in full while he does not fulfil theirs, then a terrible ending is feared for this person. We take refuge in Allah! Yet, if you see one who has committed acts of disobedience crying, sad, heart-broken and humbled, falling at the feet of the righteous and visiting them, and acknowledging his shortcomings, then a good ending is hoped for such a person.

A guide to Allah is rare

If you look for a *qārī* [an expert reciter of the Qur'an], you will find a countless number; if you seek a doctor, you will find many;

and if you seek a jurist, you will find a similarly large amount; but if you were to look for someone who can guide you to Allah and acquaint you with your blemishes, then you will only find a few. So if you are fortunate to find one, hold on to him with both hands.

If you want to be triumphant, be in a state of utter humility. Allah ﷻ said, 'Allah gave you victory at Badr when you were weak' [Qur'an 3:123]. If you want to be given, then be in a state of total poverty: 'Alms are only for the poor and the destitute' [Qur'an 9:60].

You are in the middle of a river, yet thirsty. You are with Him in His presence, yet seek connection with Him. It is as if slaves did not continue their journey together to the Hereafter except by a great deal of eating and drinking. Were they told that this [behaviour] would deliver them to the Hereafter? Look how cheaply you view your self! Were it not contemptuous in your eyes, you would not have exposed it to Allah's torment ﷻ. Yet, how precious it is [in your estimation] when seeking this world and amassing it! What is truly amazing is someone who asks an astrologer about his condition, yet does not ask the Book of Allah and the Sunnah of Allah's Messenger ﷺ.

If you become too frail to worship, mend your worship with weeping and pleading.

If you are asked, 'Who deserves to be cried over?' [You should] reply, 'A slave who has been given good health, yet he spends it in disobedience to Allah!'

If you sleep in a state of confusion, you will see confusion in your dreams. Instead, you should sleep in a state of purity and [after] repentance, so that He opens your heart with His light. However, whoever spends his day talking idly will be forgetful of Allah during the night.

If you see a friend of Allah ﷻ, then do not let your reverence for him stop you from sitting before him courteously and taking blessings from him.

The heavens and the earth show courtesy to a friend of Allah (walī)

Know that the heavens and the earth show courtesy to a friend of Allah, just as humans show courtesy to him. A person's stupidity is established when he rejoices at this world coming to him; but the more foolish person is he who grieves when he is deprived of it. Such a person is like someone to whom a snake comes to bite which then slithers away and Allah rescues him from it, and so he grieves over it for not having harmed him.

Your being concerned with the uncertain is a sign of heedlessness and lack of intelligence. [You concern yourself with] whether something will happen or not, yet you are unconcerned about that which will inevitably happen. You wake up in the morning and say, 'What will the price be tomorrow, and how will it be this year?' [All the time,] whilst [in this heedlessness,] Allah's grace comes from where you do not expect. Having doubt about one's provision is in reality doubt about the Provider. A thief did not steal, and an usurper did not usurp, except their own provision. As long as you are alive nothing will be diminished of your provision.

You are sufficiently ignorant to be concerned with the trivial but unconcerned about that which is important. Be concerned about whether you will you die as a Muslim or a disbeliever. Be concerned about whether you will be damned or felicitous. Be concerned about the Fire, which is described as everlasting. Be concerned about whether you will take the book [of judgement] by the right hand or the left.[39] These are the matters that you should be concerned about. Do not be concerned about the morsel that you eat or the sip that you drink. Does a [noble] king

39. The obedient believers will take their book of deeds in their right hands, as opposed to the unbelievers who will take it with their left. See the Qur'an, 'As for the one given his book in his right hand...' (69:19).

employ you and not feed you? Do you find yourself in the house of hospitality yet feel neglected [by the host]?

The most beloved of things by which Allah is obeyed is trust in Him.

For you to be obscure in this world is better than for you to be obscure on the Day of Resurrection.

The [following is the] quintessence of [the meaning of] one's life and its sieve: O the one who only eats threshed wheat, no doubt your deeds will be threshed, such that nothing will remain for you except that in which you were sincere, and everything apart from that shall be discarded. What is most feared for you is mingling with people. As if it was not enough that you listen [to them] with your ears, but you actually join them in backbiting, which nullifies one's ablution and breaks one's fast.[40]

You are sufficiently ignorant to be protective over your wife but not protective over your faith. It is treacherous that you are protective over her for yourself, yet you are not protective over your heart which is your Lord's. If you were to protect that which is yours, why do you not protect that which is your Lord's?

If you see someone who wakes up in the morning worried about his provision, then know that he is remote from Allah, because if a human being, who is only created, was to tell him not to work tomorrow because he would give him five dirhams, then you would see that he would trust him, despite him being an impoverished created being. So are you not satisfied with the Rich, the Generous, the One who has guaranteed you your sustenance throughout your lifespan?

A poet has said:

> When the twentieth of Sha'bān has passed, then continue
> Drinking throughout the night and day.

---

40. Such actions do not literally nullify one's fast or ablution, but rather the reward for these acts is diminished.

> And do not drink in small cups, for time has become too
> Constricted for [drinking in] small [cups].

The meaning of it, according to him, is that when the twentieth of Sha'bān has passed, then Ramadan, which will end our drinking [during the day], is imminent. Its meaning according to the people of the spiritual path is that when you have left behind forty years, then continually do righteous actions night and day, because the time has come close to [your] meeting Allah ﷻ; and your deeds are not like that of a young person who has not wasted his youth and vigour like you did.

Suppose you want to be assiduous, but your strength does not assist you; in that case, you must do righteous deeds according to your state and mend the rest with the remembrance [of Allah], because there is nothing easier than the latter: it is possible for you while standing, sitting, reclining and when sick. The Messenger of Allah ﷺ said, 'Let your tongue be moist with the remembrance of Allah.'[41] Remain persistent with whichever invocation or formula of remembrance is easy for you, because its succour comes from Allah ﷻ. You were only able to remember Him through His benevolence [to you]; and you did not turn away from Him except by His overwhelming force and dominance. Therefore, work and strive, because being oblivious in one's works is better than being totally devoid [of them].[42]

---

41. Al-Tirmidhī narrated it (3375) and graded it as authentic (*ḥasan*) with the wording, 'Verily, a man said, "O Messenger of Allah, the laws of Islam have become too much for me, so inform me of something that I can adhere to." He replied, "Let your tongue remain moist with the remembrance of Allah ﷻ."'

42. The author says in aphorism 48 of his *Ḥikam*, 'Do not forsake remembrance [of Allah] due to your lack of presence with Allah therein, because your obliviousness from His remembrance is worse than your obliviousness during His remembrance.'

Your state appears to be of those abstinent in [seeking Allah's] bounty; that is because a seeker does not cease knocking on doors; rather, you find him ever standing at them. In such a case, he is like a mother whose child has died: do you see her attending weddings, celebrations and festivities? On the contrary, she is preoccupied with the loss of her child.

How often does the Master send you His bounties, yet you behave like a fugitive slave, such that your similitude is like that of a baby in a cot: whenever he is rocked, he falls asleep. If a king was to send you a gift, you would not wake up in the morning except at his door. So take advantage of time [that allows] for acts of obedience and be steadfast therein.

If you seek to disobey Him, look for a place in which no one sees you, and look for strength to disobey Him from someone else. You will not be able to do so, because everything is from His blessings. Do you take His blessings and disobey Him through them? Nay, you have become seasoned in your violations [of Allah's commandments]: sometimes by backbiting, sometimes by tale-bearing and at other times by looking [at the unlawful]; that which you have built over seventy years you demolish in one breath.

O destroyer of acts of obedience, Allah did not afflict you with poverty and need except for you to resort to Him and for you to devote yourself to Him. O you who drowns himself in base desires and acts of disobedience, if only you gave it [i.e. your self] that which is from the lawful. How can you not love Him when you treat Him with ignobility, while He treats you with benevolence? How can you not love Him who treats you with benevolence, while you treat Him callously?

No one accompanies you to benefit you; everyone who accompanies you only does so for himself. Your wife only loves you in order to reap from you the good things in life and clothing. This is also true of your child, for he says, 'I support myself through you'; and then when you grow old and no longer have any strength, not even a residue,[43] they discard you!

If you were to dissociate yourself from creation, Allah ﷻ would open for you the door to intimacy with Him, because Allah's friends have subdued themselves through solitude and isolation. Thereafter, they heard from Allah and found intimacy with Him. So if you wish to extract the mirror of your heart from sludge, refuse what they have refused: the enjoyment of intimacy with creation and gossip. Furthermore, do not sit at the gates of neighbourhoods, because whoever prepares himself will attain support. If you were facilitated in preparing yourself, then the door to seeking succour would have been opened for you. Whoever knows how to correctly knock on the door, it will be opened for him. Many a seeker did not know how to correctly knock on the door and thus was refused [entry] because of his poor manners, and so it was not opened for him.

Slaves are vulnerable to falling flat on their faces due to their lack of silence. Had you drawn near to Allah,[44] you would have always heard Him addressing [you],[45] in your market and in your house. Whoever wakes up will witness; and whoever falls asleep, the ears of his heart will not hear and his insight will not witness; but the veil is draped [for those who seek to witness].[46]

---

43. In another edition it reads '*bughyah* [objective or use]' instead of '*baqiyyah* [residue]'.

44. In another edition it reads 'if you had fled to Allah'.

45. [SM] That is, He would send His inspirations (*wāridāt*) to your heart so as to direct you to His Oneness; and these are internal inspirations that directly enter the hearts, as opposed to external inspirations that occur on the tongues of creation whereby one understands from Allah.

46. [SM] In other words, the veil does not exist, as the Real is not veiled; rather, the veil only exists in the slave's imagination. Therefore, it is his imagination that veils him from the Real, and so if he was to raise the illusion of there being anything [independently] existent alongside the Real, then the veil would be lifted.

If the slaves [of Allah] were astute, they would not have devoted themselves to other than Allah, nor would they have sat in front of other than Him. And neither would they have sought judgement (*fatwa*) from other than Him, due to his words ﷺ, 'Seek judgement from your heart, even if they issue you a legal judgement [in its favour].' Because inspired thoughts[47] come from Allah ﷻ, so they are in conformity [with Allah's pleasure], whereas the legal expert [*mufti*] may err. The heart is not prone to error; but this [ability to understand reality] is exclusively for pure hearts. Only a [true] scholar is sought for legal judgement; as for the one who [appears to be a scholar but] is oblivious of Allah ﷻ, then he has no knowledge.

The miracles of the Prophet's ﷺ Companions ﷺ

They [the Companions] ﷺ would not embark upon anything for the sake of their selves; rather, [they would act] for Allah and with [the help of] Allah. The distance between the friends of Allah and the Companions [of the Prophet ﷺ] has grown remote, so the miracles [that are bestowed upon the friends of Allah] have been given as a consolation for their lack of complete emulation [of the Prophet ﷺ]. Some people say, 'The friends of Allah have been blessed with miracles, while the Companions were not.' On the contrary, the latter received tremendous miracles by virtue of their accompanying him ﷺ. Indeed what miracle is greater than it?

The beneficial prayer

Know that any [outwardly performed] prayer that does not thereafter restrain its performer from indecency, and reprehensible words and deeds, is not called a prayer because of His words ﷻ, 'Verily, prayer restrains from indecency and vile deeds

47. In another edition it reads 'divine thoughts'.

(*munkar*)' [Qur'an 29:45]. You come out of the prayer and your intimate discourse with the Real ﷻ with His words ﷻ, 'It is You that we worship, and it is You from whom we seek help' [Qur'an 1:5]; and [you come out of] your intimate discourse with the Messenger ﷺ with your words, 'Peace be upon you, O Prophet, and the mercy of Allah and His blessings'; and this is in every prayer. Then you leave [the prayer] to commit sins after having these blessings bestowed upon you by Allah?

Shaykh Abū al-Ḥasan al-Shādhilī relates that the Islamic jurists (*fuqahā'*) of Alexandria and its judge would come to him. One day, they came to test the Shaykh, and he sensed [*tafarrasa*] that in them. Thereupon he said, 'O jurists, O jurists! Have you ever prayed?' They replied, 'O Shaykh, does anyone of us miss prayer?' He replied to them, 'Allah ﷻ said, "Indeed, man was created anxious; fretful when afflicted by evil, and niggardly when he receives some good, except those who pray" [Qur'an 70:19–22]. When anything harmful afflicts you, do you not panic? If some good comes your way, do you not withhold it?' They were speechless. The Shaykh then said to them, 'Have you never performed this type of prayer?'

If He graces you with the ability to repent and you subsequently repent to Him, then that is out of His grace ﷻ. You commit sins for seventy years and then, when you repent to Him, in one breath He erases everything you had done in that period [before repentance]. [It has been narrated] 'Whoever repents from a sin is like someone who has not sinned.' Whenever a believer remembers his sin, he is saddened; and whenever he remembers his acts of obedience, he is elated.

Luqmān the Sage said, 'A believer has two hearts: one with which he hopes, and the other with which he fears. He hopes for his deeds to be accepted and fears that they may not be accepted. If the fear of a believer and his hope were to be weighed, they would be in a state of equilibrium.'

Whoever wants to be totally absorbed in Allah, then he should discharge Allah's commandments.

If you realise that your wife has been unfaithful, you will be infuriated with her. Similarly, your self has been unfaithful to you throughout your life. Intelligent people unanimously agree that if a wife is unfaithful, then her husband does not accommodate her but rather divorces her; so divorce your self.

The reasons for entry into Paradise and the Hellfire

The Messenger of Allah ﷺ was asked, 'What is the main reason for people entering Paradise?' He ﷺ replied, 'God-consciousness (*taqwā*) and good character.' Whereupon he was asked, 'So what is the main reason for people entering the Fire?' He ﷺ replied, 'The two cavities: the mouth and the genitalia.' Therefore, wash your heart with remorse for what Allah ﷻ has deprived you.

They were wrong – by Allah – in holding assemblies of women to lament over their wives and husbands, parents and children. Instead, they should have rightly held assemblies of women to lament over their hearts lacking God-consciousness.

Do you laugh out loud as if you have passed over the bridge (*ṣirāṭ*) [on the Day of Resurrection] and have crossed over the fires?

If you do not have scrupulousness before Allah that deters you from committing acts of disobedience to Allah when you are alone, then throw soil over your head. This is because he ﷺ said, 'Whoever has no scrupulousness that deters him from acts of disobedience to Allah when he is alone, then Allah does not care for his works.'

There is nothing that will disgrace you on the Day of Resurrection like a dirham you spent on something unlawful.[48]

48. In another edition it reads 'There is nothing that will benefit you on the Day of Resurrection like a dirham that you spent on something lawful'.

It is not important that someone is nice to you when you agree with him; but, rather, what is [really] important is that someone is nice to you when you differ with him.

The deficiency is in you and so is the veil

It is greatly feared that you will commit incessant sins whereby He beguiles you and empowers you to do them. Allah ﷻ said, 'We shall beguile them from where they do not know' [Qur'an 68:44].

If He cares for you, then a small amount will suffice you; but if He does not care for you, then a large amount [of anything] will not avail you.

If the veil was lifted for you, you would have seen everything glorifying (*tasbīḥ*) Allah ﷻ. However, the deficiency is in you, and the veil is from you.

How protective you are over your body, yet how cheap your religion is to you! If you were told, 'This food is poisoned,' you would refrain from [eating] it. Furthermore, if someone else was to swear that it is not poisoned on an oath to divorce his wife [if he was lying], you would still refrain from it. Rather, even if you were to repeatedly wash the utensil in which it is in, you would still be repulsed by it. So why are you not like that with regard to your religion?

How many more favours Allah has over you than your mother! When she takes you as a baby, she dresses you in the finest clothes; and if you defile them, she will change them immediately. Yet you come to an embellished kingdom, wherein there is not a space of a hand span except that it is fit to prostrate on, and you ruin your clothes and defile them with disobedience. Your deeds are such: beautiful ornaments are manifested before you, and you defile them with acts of disobedience!

Not everyone who has accompanied the great ones was guided by accompanying them. So do not consider the accompanying of shaykhs to be a pretext for your feeling safe and secure. Whoever is duped with regard to Allah has disobeyed Him; that is because you have assured yourself safety from His punishment. Just as an ignoramus says, 'I have accompanied my master [*sayyidī*] So-and-so, and I have seen my master So-and-so,' and they make claims: all of them untrue and false. Instead, their accompanying the shaykhs should have increased them in fear and dread, for the Companions accompanied the Messenger of Allah ﷺ and, as a result, they were the most fearful and terrified.

It may be that affluence is a cause for one to turn away [from Allah] and poverty a cause for devotion [to Allah], because poverty compels one to beseech Allah. Therefore, poverty that causes you to be devoted to Allah is better than affluence which severs you from Him.

Just as you have been commanded to avoid acts of disobedience, you have also been commanded to avoid someone disobedient [to Allah], whilst privately praying for him. People, today, are the opposite. How likely is it that your fasts and prayers will be of any benefit to you when you malign your Muslim brother?

Renewal of faith

He ﷺ said, 'Renew your faith with the words "There is no god except Allah".' This demonstrates that one is subjected to the dust of disobedience and the filth of opposition [to Him], and that not every impurity is purified by water. In fact, many an impurity is only purified by fire, just like gold when there is impurity in it. Likewise the disobedient from this nation are not fit to enter Paradise until they are purified by the Fire.

No one is to be envied except a slave who has been wrapped in the garment of God-consciousness. This is the real life, and what a fine life it is for the lover with the Beloved when no one is observing him! If he wants someone to observe him, then he is not genuine in his love. If anyone wants others to be aware of his state, then [know that] he has been deceived.

Do not be like worldly-minded people whom the world has divorced. Rather, be from amongst those who have divorced it and detached themselves from it before their separation. If you prefer this world over the Hereafter, then you are similar to someone who has two wives: one of them is an unfaithful old woman, and the other a faithful young woman – if you prefer an unfaithful old woman over a faithful young woman, then are you not a fool?

He may sometimes ordain for you to commit a sin in order to rid you of pride and conceit, for it has been related, 'Many a sin has caused its perpetrator to enter Paradise.'[49] A man can pray two cycles of prayer and then depend and rely on them, and is conceited about them – this is a good deed encompassed by bad deeds. In contrast, there can be another person who commits an act of disobedience which engenders in him humility and brokenness, and makes him forever abased and needy – this is a bad deed encompassed by good deeds.

You are sufficiently ignorant to pay attention to someone else's minor offence while ignoring your own major offence.

Do not criticise people according to the ostensive [mandates] of the Sacred Law (Shariah) nor condemn them. If people today were to be charged to undertake what the Companions and the early righteous community were charged with, then they would not be able to bear it, because those [i.e. the Companions and early Muslim community] were Allah's proofs over His creation.[50]

---

49. The author says in his *Ḥikam*, 'Many an act of disobedience that has bequeathed humiliation and impoverishment is better than an act of obedience that has bequeathed haughtiness and arrogance.'

50. [SM] The condition of people today varies from those of the Companions ﷺ, since the good deeds of the righteous (*ḥasanāt al-abrār*) are the bad deeds of those intimate with Allah (*sayyi'āt al-muqarrabīn*). This is why Abū Sa'īd al-Khudrī said to some of the *tābi'īn* [the followers of the Compnaions], 'You do deeds that are finer [i.e. insignificant] in your eyes than hair, which we would consider during the Messenger of Allah's time ﷺ

The people of insight see this world (*dunyā*)[51] as a carcass in which dogs have stuck their noses. Tell me, if a man was to dip his mouth into a carcass, would you not consider him despicable? If the Real ﷻ has established a scale for buying and selling, then has He not established a scale for [weighing] realities?

Someone whose feet are impure is not fit for his heart's presence [with Allah], so what about the one whose mouth is impure?

Whoever proves to be treacherous is humiliated. The value of a hand is five hundred dinars,[52] but if it proves to be treacherous, then it is amputated for the sake of a quarter of a dinar. Whoever dares to commit a minor sin falls into a major one.

Know the hidden motives of your lower self and do not trust it. If it tells you to visit So-and-so, then [fear that] maybe you will be going to a blazing fire, deliberately casting yourself therein. These [times] are only times for socialising; rarely do you sit amongst people without disobeying Allah therein. This is why many of the early Muslims preferred to sit in their homes and left the congregational prayer. If your self demands you to go out, then busy it at home with some act of obedience,

---

as being from the destructive sins (*mūbiqāt*).' Accordingly, one needs to treat people according to their potential; so we don't condemn them for falling into a sub-optimal (*khilāf al-awlā*) or disliked (*makrūh*) action in the same manner as we would condemn them for falling into the unlawful (*ḥarām*), as this is something which should be condemned. We therefore judge [others] with leniency and dispensation (*rukhṣah*), while holding ourselves accountable with severity and stringency (*'azīmah*).

51. In another edition it reads 'a sin (*al-dhanb*)' instead of 'this world (*al-dunyā*)'.

52. The prescribed legal punishment (*ḥadd*) of amputation of a thief's hand is subject to stringent conditions for the theft of something to the value of quarter of a dinar. There is, however, a difference of opinion amongst the jurists with regards to the details of this ruling. But the value of the hand, in terms of its indemnity, if someone cut or paralysed someone else's hand, is five hundred dinars.

because backbiting is worse than thirty adulteries in Islam. Dogs, however, do not sleep in high-walled villas[53] but instead sleep on rubbish heaps.

Whoever wants to look at the similitude of hearts, then let him look at dwellings where [one finds that] there is a house that is inhabited, and another that is in ruins, such that the latter remains a place for people to use as a lavatory. Likewise there is a heart like a prosperous shop, and a heart like a shop in ruins.

Whoever is honest with Allah, He will guard him against harm from his enemies

You will not be purified[54] until you attend to Allah [as He is entitled to servitude over one's lower self]. Therefore, donate some charity every day, even if it is with a quarter of a dirham or a morsel, so that Allah may record your name in the register of the charitable. Moreover, recite a portion of the Qur'an every day, even if it is one verse, so that Allah may record your name in the register of the Qur'an reciters. Then pray during the night, even if it is only two cycles, so that Allah may record your name with those who stand for prayer. Do not err and say, 'Whoever has just enough food for each day, how can he be expected to donate charity?' Allah ﷻ said, 'Let the rich spend of their wealth, and whoever's wealth is constricted for him, then let him spend some of what Allah has given him' [Qur'an 65:7]. The poor person who is given charity is like a mount that carries your provisions to the Hereafter.

Whoever wants [to reach] the advanced stages [of the spiritual path], let him rectify the preliminary stages.

Whoever is honest with Allah, Allah will protect him against harm from his enemies and will relieve him of the need for

53. In another edition it reads 'do not sleep on walls'.
54. In another edition it reads 'your sun shall appear'.

aides,[55] because the one who is in need of creation is utterly humiliated.

Do you think that medicine is sweet?[56] If you do not force it down, you will not be cured. So force repentance down yourself and do not let the sweetness of disobedience prevail over you. If you perceive yourself craving a base desire, then flee to Allah and seek help from Him, for He will rescue you from it.

Instead of saying, 'Where are the people of *khaṭwā*?[57] Where are the friends [of Allah]? Where are the real men?' [You should] say, 'Where is the insight?' Is someone smeared with faeces fit to see the sultan's daughter?

It has been related that Shaykh Makīn al-Dīn al-Asmar ﷺ said, 'I was in Alexandria when suddenly I saw a sun that had risen alongside the sun. I was amazed at that, so I came close to it and lo and behold it was a young boy whose sideburns had grown. His light prevailed over the light of the sun. I greeted him, so he replied to my greeting of peace. Then I asked him, "Where are you from?" He replied, "I performed the dawn prayer (*fajr*) at Masjid al-Aqṣa in Jerusalem, and I will perform the noon prayer (*ẓuhr*) with you, the late afternoon prayer (*'aṣr*) in Mecca and the sunset prayer (*maghrib*) in Medina!" So I asked him, "Will you be my guest?" He replied, "That is not possible." He then bade me farewell and departed.'

Whoever honours a believer, it is as if he has honoured Allah. Yet, whoever hurts a believer, it is as if he has hurt his leader and master. So beware of hurting a believer, for your self is filled with its own faults, and they are enough for you to be concerned about.

---

55. In another edition it reads 'Allah will protect him against the harm from [making] claim and relieve him of the burden of ailments'.

56. In another edition it reads 'a sweet dish that you consume'.

57. These are Allah's friends who have been given the ability to miraculously travel long distances within moments where their steps are the distance of their sight.

You are similar to an onion: when it is peeled, it emerges all as shells.[58] If you want to purify water, you cut off defiling elements from it. Your limbs are like rivulets that flow to the heart. So beware of irrigating your heart with bad water, such as backbiting, talebearing and obscene speech, looking at that which is unlawful and so forth, because the heart is not veiled by that which emerges from it; rather, it is only veiled by that which is resident therein. Thus, the illumination of the heart is by consuming the lawful, engaging in the remembrance of Allah, reciting the Qur'an and guarding it from looking at the lawful, disliked and unlawful created beings. Therefore, do not let loose the hunter of your sight except [on a mission] to increase in knowledge or wisdom. Instead of saying, 'This mirror is covered with rust,' say, 'There is inflammation in my eyes.'

You have love for leadership, fame and so on, yet you say, 'The shaykh does not capture our hearts.' [Instead you should] say, 'The obstacle is from me.'

If you were prepared on the first day, then you would not have needed to attend a second session. You only needed continual repetition because of the solidity of the rust over your heart, so that each session served as a polish.

You need to seek all of your needs from your Master and leave those who cannot benefit others.

Make definite your despair of creation,[59] and direct your hopes towards the True King, and look at the state of your deeds and

---

58. [SM] The author makes the comparison between an onion and a person's lower self: just as an onion is all layers, and if you want to get rid of the onion, then you rid it of its layers. Likewise, the self is full of blameworthy traits, so if you want to get rid of the blameworthy traits, you need to get rid of your lower self; as Imam al-Rifā'ī said, 'Leave your self and come,' and Shaykh Arsalān al-Dimashqī said, 'All of you is hidden polytheism (*shirk*) and the Divine Oneness will not be made clear to you until you leave your self.'

59. Aḥmad narrated (23540) with an authentic chain of transmission on the authority of Abū Ayyūb al-Anṣārī ﵁ that he said, 'A man came to

how He has treated you from the beginning of your childhood. He has only treated you with generosity and kindness. Then look at how you have treated Him, and you will only find insolence and disobedience.

How frequently you befriend creation, yet how seldom you seek to befriend Allah!

Allah is the king, you are the shepherd and your limbs are your sheep

Your limbs are your sheep, your heart[60] is the shepherd, and Allah is the King. If you graze them in a fertile pasture until you have pleased the King, then you deserve His approval. But if, on the other hand, you graze them in unwholesome pasture until most of them become frail and feeble, and then a wolf comes and devours some of them, then you deserve to be punished by the King. If He wishes, He exacts His retribution from you; and if He wishes, He pardons you. Hence, your limbs are either doors to Paradise or doors to the Fire.[61] If you utilise them for that which is pleasing to Him, then you are walking progressively on the path to Paradise, otherwise you are walking progressively on the path to the Fire. These are the scales of wisdom, so weigh with them your intelligence just as you weigh with them tangible things. If you want to know how to cross the bridge [on the Day of Resurrection], then look at your state in hastening to the mosques. The recompense for someone who comes to the

---

the Prophet ﷺ and said, "Admonish me and be brief." So he replied, "When you stand to perform your prayer, then perform the prayer of someone bidding farewell; and do not say something for which you need to apologise; and completely despair of what is in people's hands [i.e. their wealth and possessions].'"

60. In another edition it reads 'you are the shepherd'.

61. In another edition it reads 'either reward to Paradise, or either your punishment to Hellfire'.

mosque before the call for prayer [*adhān*] is that he will cross the bridge like a flash of lightning; whereas someone who comes at the beginning of the [prayer] time shall pass over it like a racehorse.

The path of uprightness is not perceived by the eyes but rather by the hearts. Allah ﷻ said, 'And this is My path, which is straight, so follow it' [Qur'an 6:153]. He did not point [with His word *this*] except to something that exists. So for whomsoever the path is illuminated, he should follow it, and for whomsoever the path is dark, he will not perceive it and will therefore remain perplexed. If you have given free rein to your hearing, sight and tongue during your life, then restrain now what you have let loose. The Messenger of Allah ﷺ said, 'The poor believers will enter Paradise five hundred years before the wealthy.' That is because they outstripped [others] in this world with acts of worship, whereas you miss the congregational prayer and pray alone; and when you do perform it, you do so like the pecking of a cockerel. Should the gifts given to kings be anything other than the finest and most carefully selected? The poor only outstripped [others] to Paradise because they outstripped others in serving the Master in this world. What is meant by the poor here are those who are patient with the bitterness of poverty, such that one of them rejoices at adversity just as you rejoice at prosperity. Therefore, the poor entering Paradise before the rich demonstrates their patience with poverty.

You are sufficiently ignorant to frequent creation and leave the door of the Creator! You have committed every act of disobedience under the sun, so are you not saddened at your state?

The manner of keeping company

It is truly amazing that a slave who is avid in accompanying his lower self, while only evil comes from it, will at the same time forsake accompanying Allah, while only goodness comes from Him.

If it is said, 'How does one accompany Allah?' then know that accompanying anything is relative to that thing: accompanying Allah ﷻ is by complying with His commandments and avoiding His prohibitions; accompanying the two angels is by dictating to them good deeds; accompanying the Book and the Sunnah is by acting in accordance with them; accompanying the skies is by reflecting over them; and accompanying the earth is by pondering over what is on it.

It is not from the necessary consequences of accompanying [something or someone] that one be on an equal rank [with it]. The meaning of accompanying Allah is accompanying His favours and blessings. So whoever accompanies blessings with gratitude, accompanies tribulations with patience, accompanies [His] commandments with compliance, [accompanies] His prohibitions with avoidance and obedience with sincerity, then he has truly accompanied Allah ﷻ. Then, when companionship is strengthened, it turns to intimate friendship.

Beware of saying that goodness has disappeared and its rug has been rolled up. We do not want someone to cause people to despair of Allah's mercy and render them hopeless of Him ﷻ, for [it is mentioned] in the Psalms of Dāwūd (upon him and our Prophet be the best of blessings and salutations), 'I am most merciful to My slave when he turns away from Me: since many an obedient person has been destroyed by conceit, and many a sinner was forgiven because of his heartbreak [over his sins].'

It has been related that Shaykh Makīn al-Dīn al-Asmar said, 'I saw in Alexandria a slave with his master, and over them there was a flag which had covered that which is between the sky and the earth. I said [to myself], "Does this flag belong to the master or the slave?" I decided to follow them until his master bought him a need of his and left him. Then when the slave disappeared, the flag disappeared with him, so I realised that he was one of the friends of Allah ﷻ. I went over to his master and said to him, "Will you sell me this slave?" He replied, "Why?" He persisted [in wanting to know the reason for my interest] until I mentioned to him the affair of his slave. He then said to me, "O my master, what you are seeking, I am more in need of it."[62] He then set him free. He [i.e. the slave] was a great friend of Allah.'

There are amongst them those who know the friends of Allah by smelling without the presence of perfume, and amongst them those who know them by tasting: when he sees a friend of Allah, he can taste sweetness in his mouth, and whenever he sees someone who is severed [from Allah], he can taste bitterness in his mouth.

Whoever does not forsake the unlawful things, his undertaking the necessary duties will be of no avail to him. Whoever does not take preventative measures, then medicine is of no benefit to him.

How little is the blessing in wealth which falls in the hands of plunderers! Understand this – by Allah – the lives of the heedless are plundered.

The similitude of this world is like that of a decrepit old leper woman who is concealed by a silk dress. A believer is repulsed and repulses others from her because of her exposing herself before him. No one has worn a garment more foul than the garment of claim, such that he says during an argument, 'Are you like me? Are you worthy of speaking to me? Are you worthy of me speaking to you!' The first to be destroyed by this was Iblīs. Beware of this, even if he [who is speaking to you] is a lame scabby leper; do not despise him, because of the sanctity of 'There is no god except Allah' that is in his heart. Give everyone the benefit of doubt, and you shall be successful.

Do you think that good character is for a person to be amicable and from the most generous of people, yet to be

62. [SM] In other words, you want to buy him so that you may free him, but I am more entitled to him than you after you have acquainted me with his reality and I have now realised his worth, so how can I sell him to you? Therefore, I will be the one to free him.

neglectful of the rights of Allah ﷻ? This is not good character. On the contrary, a slave is not praised with having good character until he undertakes the rights of Allah ﷻ, implements His rulings, surrenders to Allah's commandments and avoids His prohibitions. Whoever therefore restrains himself from committing acts of disobedience to Allah and fulfils Allah's rights is of good character.

Allah has not compelled the tongues of the slaves against you except for you to return to Him. Do you not see that you continue to be valuable in Allah's sight until you disobey [Him]. Then when you disobey [Him], you become worthless.

The reality of God-consciousness (taqwā)

God-consciousness is to forsake disobedience to Allah when no one sees you.

When the Prophet ﷺ used to drink water, he would say, 'All praise is due to Allah who has made it fresh and sweet out of His mercy and did not make it saline and hot due to our sins.' He ﷺ is immune from committing sins, but [he said it] out of humility and to teach [us]. It was possible for him to say, 'Due to your sins.' He ﷺ did not eat or drink except to teach us the correct etiquette, because he ﷺ used to be fed and given drink.[63] A gnostic tilts his head downwards when he drinks – and maybe his eyes shed tears – and says, 'This is affection from Allah ﷻ.'

Some of them would not leave home for the congregational prayer because of what they were exposed to en route; amongst them was Mālik ibn Anas ؓ. That is because the congregational prayer is profit, and profit is only accounted for after complete coverage of the capital.

---

63. Al-Bukhārī (1762) and Muslim (1104) narrated that he ﷺ said, 'Verily, I am not like you; I spend the night with One who feeds me and gives me drink.' In the narration of Muslim it reads, 'Verily, my Lord feeds me and gives me drink.'

Do not think that predators are [only found] in jungles. On the contrary, there are predators in the markets and streets, and they are those things which tear up the hearts.

The similitude of someone who constantly commits sins and seeks forgiveness is like someone who constantly drinks poison and takes its antidote. He should be told, 'There may come an occasion when you are unable to get to the antidote [in time] and thus death will seize you by surprise before you can get to it.'

Whoever has a diseased heart is deprived of wearing the garment of God-consciousness. If your heart was not corrupted with the disease of caprice and base desires, you would have been able to bear the burdens of God-consciousness. Whoever does not taste the sweetness of obedience, it indicates that there is a disease in his heart due to base desires. Allah has called base desires a disease in His words ﷻ, 'So the one who has a disease in his heart covets' [Qur'an 33:32]. You have two methods in treating it: utilising that which is beneficial for you, namely acts of obedience; and avoiding that which is harmful to you, namely acts of disobedience. If you commit a sin and follow it up with repentance, remorse, heartbreak and penitence [to Allah], then that will be a means for your reuniting with Him. But if you do an act of obedience and follow it up with conceit and arrogance, then that will be a means for your severance from Him.

How strange it is that you want to improve your heart, yet your limbs do whatever unlawful actions they want, such as gazing [at the unlawful], backbiting, talebearing and so forth! Hence, your similitude is like that of someone who treats himself with poison or someone who wants to clean his garment with soot.

The necessity of isolating and secluding yourself

You need to seclude and isolate yourself. Whoever adopts solitude as a habit, he shall attain honour. Then, whosoever's solitude is genuine, he shall attain gifts from the Real as favours. Its signs are:

1. the uncovering of the veil;
2. revitalisation of the heart;
3. and the realisation of love.

Therefore, you should be concerned with the quality of your deeds and not their quantity. The similitude of many deeds lacking quality is like that of many cheap clothes; and the similitude of a few deeds of good quality is like that of a few valuable clothes. [Thus a few good deeds of a high quality are] just like an emerald: small in size but invaluable. Thus whoever occupies his heart with Allah, and treats its caprices, is better than someone who performs many prayers and fasts [whilst inattentive].

The similitude of someone who performs the prayer without presence of heart is like someone who gives a king a hundred empty boxes as a gift; [in reality,] he deserves to be punished by the king. As for someone who performs it with presence of heart, then he is like someone who gives the king a ruby worth a thousand dinars as a gift: the king will always remember him [fondly] for it.

The person praying is intimately conversing with Allah and His Messenger ﷺ

When you enter the prayer, you are intimately conversing with Allah ﷻ and speaking to His Messenger ﷺ, because you say, 'Peace be upon you, O Prophet, and Allah's mercy and His blessings,' and it is not said, 'O So-and-so,' according to the Arabs except to someone who is present.

Two cycles of prayer at night are better than a thousand during the day. You will not perform two cycles of prayer during it except you will find them in your scale [of good deeds]. Is a slave purchased for any purpose other than to serve?[64] Have you seen a slave who is bought to eat and sleep? You are nothing but a slave who has been purchased. Allah ﷻ said, 'Indeed, Allah has purchased from the believers themselves and their wealth in exchange for Paradise; they fight in the way of Allah, and so they kill and are killed' [Qur'an 9:111].

Whoever does not compel his self, it will latch on to him; and whoever does not demand from it, it will demand from him. If you burden it with acts of obedience, it will not demand acts of disobedience from you nor will it find an opportunity to commit them. Have you seen the righteous and the devotees spectating at festivities? Whoever occupies his self with the lawful things and amusement will be preoccupied from standing at night [in prayer], and so it will be said to him, 'You have occupied yourself away from Us, so We will occupy you from worshipping Us.'

Two cycles of prayer in the middle of the night are heavier for you than the mountain of Uḥud. Limbs that have dried up from performing acts of obedience are only fit for severance; for a tree, when it dries up, is only fit for the fire.

Whoever loves this world with his heart is like someone who has built a beautiful building above which is a toilet that leaks on it and continues to do so until its exterior appears the same as its interior. Amongst them there are those who clean it so that his heart remains white. Its cleansing is by repentance, invocations (*adhkār*), remorse and seeking forgiveness. Similarly, you are in Allah's proximity (*haḍrah*), defiled by your disobedience [to Him]: you consume the unlawful and look at the unlawful. Whoever commits violations and [submits to] base desires, his heart is darkened. If you do not repent while you are healthy, He may afflict you with ailments and calamities so that you may be purified from all sins, just like a washed garment. Therefore,

64. In another edition it reads 'do you purchase a slave'.

polish the mirror of your heart with solitude and remembrance until you meet Allah ﷻ. Let it be a single formula of remembrance [that you concentrate on],[65] so that the lights may emanate from within you. Do not be like someone who wants to dig a well, and so he digs an arm's length here and an arm's length there such that no water ever springs forth for him. Instead, dig in a single place so that water may spring forth for you.

O slave of Allah, your religion is your capital; if you lose it, you have lost your capital. Therefore, busy your tongue with His remembrance, your heart with His love and your limbs in His service, and cultivate your existence until the seed [of true faith] appears and thus grows. Whoever treats his heart in the way a farmer treats his land, his heart will be illuminated.

The similitude [of the spiritual path] is like that of two men who bought equally proportionate land. One of them took it and cleared it of thorns and grass, irrigated it with water and sowed its seeds until they grew; he harvested and benefited from it. This person is like someone who grew up in obedience [to Allah], such that the lights of his heart have illuminated. As for the other person, he neglected it until thorns and grass grew on it and it thus remained a shelter for snakes and lizards; this person is someone whose heart became dark by acts of disobedience.

If you attend a gathering [of remembrance or admonishment] and leave to commit violations and acts of heedlessness, then beware of saying, 'How does my attendance benefit me?' Rather, [you must simply continue to] attend; you may have had a [spiritual] disease for forty years, so do you expect it to disappear from you in a moment or in a day? This case is similar to that of sand that has been thrown in one place for forty years; do you expect it to disappear in a moment or in a day? Whoever commits acts of disobedience and tosses and turns in unlawful activity

65. In another edition it reads 'let your heart make remembrance'.

will not be purified, even if he was immersed in the seven oceans, until he resolves to repent to Allah.

The outer and inner major ritual impurity (janābah)

The outer [body] is subject to major ritual impurity (*janābah*) which bars you from entering His house [i.e. the mosque] and reciting His Book. The inner is also subject to major ritual impurity (*janābah*) which bars you from entering His proximity and understanding His speech; and it is heedlessness.

If your lower self demands base desires, then bridal it with the bridal of the Sacred Law. It is like a beast which inclines towards someone else's crops. So lower the gaze[66] from its inclination towards delights and [lower] the heart from its inclination towards base desires, and let your heart be constantly vitalised. The Real ﷻ chose for His proximity those who are worthy of it. As for those who are unworthy, He has cast them to the creation. Their similitude is like that of slaves who were presented before the king: whomsoever the king keeps [for Himself] is honoured, and whoever is unworthy is left for the subjects [of the king].

You have not gone to a place of wisdom or disobedience except there was either a luminous chain on your neck or a dark one. If you do not perceive of it, then [know that] others do. Do you not see that the sun is witnessed by everyone except the blind?

What is the benefit of knowledge other than to act in accordance with it? Its similitude is like that of a king who wrote a letter to his deputy on the frontier – what is the purpose of the letter? For it to only be read? [Rather,] its purpose is only for you to act according to it.

---

66. In another edition it reads 'then close your eyes'.

Insight and wandering about aimlessly

A person who busies himself with seeking knowledge (*'ilm*),[67] yet does not have insight, is like a hundred thousand blind men who travel on a road utterly confused [about the way]. If there had been amongst them a one-eyed person, all of the people would have followed him and left the hundred thousand blind men behind.

The scholar who does not act in accordance with his knowledge is like a candle that gives light to people by burning itself.[68]

[If one has] knowledge but is heedless of Allah, then ignorance is better [for such a person]. Whosoever's limbs bear fruit, then his heart has given rain to its tongue by remembrance, to his eyes by closing [them], to his ears by listening to knowledge and to his hands and feet by hastening towards good.

Whoever frequently sits with the people of this age has exposed himself to disobeying Allah ﷻ. In such a case, he will be similar to someone who puts dry wood in the fire and expects it to not light up in flames; he is expecting the impossible, as the wood has fallen in.

Whoever is well known among people is distinguished by tribulations, whereas whoever does not know them has truly lived amongst them.[69] You may have sat with someone impious, though you yourself were pious, and so he dragged you towards backbiting and prevailed over your self.

Nothing has ruined hearts more than the lack of fear [of Allah]. A good heart is that which is not distracted from Allah by the

---

67. In another edition it reads 'performing deeds (*'amal*)' instead of 'seeking knowledge (*'ilm*)'.

68. In another edition it reads 'The same similitude of knowledge without action is like a candle'.

69. In another edition it reads 'Whoever was acquainted with people and lived amongst them is not like someone who was unacquainted with them'.

finery [of this world]. If you want to cure your heart, then go out to the desert of repentance, and transform your state from one of absence [from Allah] to being in [His] proximity; and wear the garment of humility and poverty; then, indeed, the heart shall be cured. However, you fill your stomach and boast about being fat.[70] Thus, you are like a lamb that is fattened for slaughter; and you have surely slaughtered yourself without realising it!

Do not miss out on a gathering of wisdom, even if you happen to be committing acts of disobedience. Do not say, 'What is the benefit in listening to [what is said in] the gathering when I am unable to abandon acts of disobedience?' Instead, the archer should shoot, because if he misses the target today, he will hit it tomorrow. If you were intelligent and clever, you would have given Allah's rights precedence over your own selfish desires.

No one is made privy to secrets except a trustworthy person, yet you give your self its share of food and drink so that you may fill the toilet; are you satisfied with loving this world? Whoever loves this world has proven himself to be treacherous; and does the King make whomsoever proves to be treacherous privy to His secrets? So use the formulas of invocation, and it is upon Him to send down the lights.

Nothing benefits the heart quite like solitude in which it enters the arena of reflection. How is a heart supposed to be illuminated when the images of created beings are reflected in its mirror; or how is it supposed to travel to Allah while it succumbs to its desires; or how can it expect to enter Allah's proximity when it is not purified from the major ritual impurity (*janābah*) of its moments of heedlessness; or how can it hope to understand the subtle secrets when it has not repented from its wrongdoings?

The source of every act of disobedience, heedlessness and forgetfulness is satisfaction with the lower self; and the source

70. This was perhaps in the author's time, but it is no longer the case now.

of every act of obedience, wakefulness and self-restraint is dissatisfaction with it.

O slave, flee from this creation to the Creator

Do not travel from one created being to another like a donkey walking around [in circles] in a mill: the one who is travelled to is the same one who one had travelled from. Instead, travel from the creation to the Creator, 'And to your Lord is the final destination' [Qur'an 53:42].

[Divine] lights are merely the mounts of the hearts and the innermost depths of the hearts (*asrār*),[71] and light is the army of the heart just as darkness is the army of the lower self. When Allah wants to give triumph to His slave, He supports him with the army of lights and severs from him the support of darkness and distractions [from Allah].[72]

The light has disclosure (*kashf*),[73] the insight (*baṣīrah*) has judgement and the heart has inclination (*iqbāl*) or aversion (*idbār*) [to things].

---

71. In other words, just as mounts deliver one to one's destination, similarly the lights [i.e. Divine inspirations] deliver the hearts to their destination, which is to enter Allah's presence ﷻ. al-Shurnūbī, *Sharḥ al-Ḥikam,* 115.

72. The light referred to in this passage is divinely bestowed knowledge in the heart, which is similar to an army that is employed by a leader to defeat his enemies. Likewise darkness, which is satanic whisperings, is the army of the lower self that is ever enjoining one to evil, whose goal is the fulfilment of base desires and transitory objectives. So there is a constant battle between such whisperings and the mind, and when Allah wants to help him in conquering his base desires, He supports his heart with lights that are like armies, or armies that are lights, and severs from him the supports that are patches of darkness. 116.

73. 'Meaning that the light that Allah casts in the heart of a sincere seeker (*murīd*), which is *al-'ilm al-ladunī* [Divinely inspired knowledge], discloses the meanings [of things], such as the goodness of obedience [to Allah] and the repugnance of disobedience [to Allah]. The insight comprehends [matters] by means of this light, just as the eyesight comprehends sensory

The exterior of created beings is deception (*ghirrah*), while their interior is a lesson of admonition (*'ibrah*).[74] The self looks towards the exterior of their deception, while the heart looks towards the interior of their admonition.

Whenever Allah alienates you from His creation, then know that He wants to open for you the door to intimacy (*uns*) with Himself.

The prayer is the place of intimate discourse and the source of sincere love (*muṣāfah*) wherein the grounds of the secrets are accommodated, and in which the rays of the lights shine. Due to the fact that He knew the presence of weakness in you, He reduced its number [from fifty to only five obligatory prayers a day], and because He knew your need for His grace, He increased its reinforcements [i.e. consecutive rewards and secrets].

People praise you for what they assume is in you, so reproach your self for what you know of it. The most ignorant person is he who ignores what he is certain of based on people's assumption of him.

Conceal mankind's opinion of you for Allah's discernment of you, and be absent from their attention to you by beholding His attention towards you.

He knew that the slaves will aspire to the manifestation of the secret of His providence, so He ﷻ said, 'He selects for His mercy whomsoever He wills; Allah is the possessor of tremendous

---

objects by means of apparent light sources, like the sun or a lamp. The heart subsequently inclines towards those matters that the insight judges to be good, such as obedience, and is averse to those matters it judges to be bad, such as disobedience; and the limbs thereby follow it [the heart], as in the hadith, "Surely, if it [the piece of flesh] is corrupt, then all of the body is corrupt; verily, it is the heart" [Narrated by al-Bukhārī and Muslim].' *Ibid.* 116–17.

74. 'Its exterior is deception, namely a cause for being deceived by them because of their beauty and splendour; and their interior is a means for one to draw a lesson of admonishment due to its ugliness and baseness. So the lower self looks towards its apparent deception and thus is deceived by it until it destroys one; whereas the heart (i.e. the intellect) looks towards its inner lesson of admonishment and takes heed from it and so is saved from its evil.' *Ibid.* 137.

grace' [Qur'an 2:105]. He knew that had He left them to it, they would have forsaken deeds out of their reliance on what has been pre-eternally ordained, so He ﷻ said, 'Surely the mercy of Allah is near to those who do good' [Qur'an 7:56]. If you want gifts to arrive at your doorstep, then correct your impoverishment and need [for Him]: 'Verily, alms are only for the poor and the destitute' [Qur'an 9:60].

There are lights that have been permitted to enter, and there are lights that have been permitted to reach. It may so happen that lights have come to you but found your heart to be filled with the images of creation (*āthār*), so they fled from whence they descended. Vacate your heart from everything other than Him, and He will fill it with gnosis and secrets.

A [true] believer is too preoccupied with extolling Allah to appreciate himself, and he is too preoccupied with Allah's rights to remember his own self-interest.

Allah has placed you in the intermediate world between His sensory realm (*mulk*) and His unseen realm (*malakūt*)[75] to let you know the grandeur of your rank amongst His creation, and [to teach you] that you are a jewel which has been encompassed by the shells of His created beings.[76]

You are with creation as long as you do not behold the Creator. When you behold Him, created beings are with you.

The intelligent person

An intelligent person is more delighted with that which endures than with that which quickly perishes. His light has glistened

75. Such matters of the unseen realm include the angels, the jinn, Paradise and the Hellfire.

76. 'His created beings (which are similar to shells that encompass a precious jewel) encompass you to serve and protect you, for Allah ﷻ has made all of His creation subservient to you for your benefit, as He ﷻ said, "And He has made subservient to you all that is in the heavens and on earth" [Qur'an 45:13].' *Ibid.* 232.

and his first signs [of acceptance] have already appeared, so he shunned this abode, turning his back on it, rejecting it, and totally disregarding it. He did not take it as a permanent abode or as a place of residence. Instead, he raised his aspiration above it to Allah ﷻ and travelled to Him, seeking His assistance in his arrival to Him. The mount of his resolve does not settle; it continues to proceed along until it kneels down in the divine proximity and the rug of intimacy, the place of *mufātaḥah* [initial address], *muwājahah* [encounter], *mujālasah* [sitting together], *muḥādathah* [conversation], *mushāhadah* [beholding] and *mulāṭafah* [congeniality].[77]

The divine proximity has become the nest of their hearts; to it they take shelter and in it they take permanent residence. If they descend to the firmament of [Allah's] rights and the land of personal interests, then that is only after permission, a firm [spiritual] footing and a deeply rooted certainty. They did not descend to the rights with bad etiquette and heedlessness, nor to their personal interests with desire and enjoyment. Rather, they entered all of that through [the assistance of] Allah, for Allah, from Allah and to Allah. Therefore, beware, my brother, of lending your ear to those who malign this group [of Allah's friends], so that you do not fall from Allah's sight [of esteem] and become worthy of His wrath, as verily these people sat with Allah in all honesty, with sincere loyalty and monitoring even their breaths with Him. They submitted their reins to Him and

---

77. Al-Shurnūbī says in his commentary on the author's *Ḥikam*, 'The place of *mufātaḥah* is the Real's calling by the meanings of His names and attributes. *Muwājahah* is the Lord tending to His slave. *Mujālasah* is constantly adhering to invoking Allah [literally, sitting with Him]. *Muḥādathah* is speaking within his own *sirr* [innermost being] with gnosis and secrets that have been disclosed unto him from his Lord. *Mushāhadah* refers to unveilings (*kashf*) in which there is no illusion (*wahm*). *Mulāṭafah* is congeniality.' *Ibid.* 251. Ibn 'Abbād says in his commentary on the author's *Ḥikam*, 'These are not known except through experience, and likewise is the case with the variations in their meanings [i.e. not known except by experience].' Ibn 'Abbād, *Sharḥ al-Ḥikam al-'Aṭā'iyyah*, 512.

cast themselves peacefully before Him, and gave up defending themselves out of modesty before their Lord. Consequently, He is the One who fights on their behalf against those who wage war against them, and the One who subdues those who try to prevail over them.

Allah has especially tried this group with His creation; in particular, [they have been tried] by the scholars. Rarely do you find anyone amongst them whose heart Allah has opened to fully accepting a particular friend of His. Instead, he will say to you, 'Yes, the friends of Allah do exist, but where are they?' Not one of them is mentioned to him, except he begins to deny that Allah has elected him; quick with the tongue in justifying [this claim], devoid of belief. Beware of someone whose description is such and flee from him as you would from a lion.

Beware of attachment to other than Allah

Shaykh Abū al-Ḥasan ﷺ said, 'A jurist (*faqīh*) is not someone whom the veil has gouged out his heart's eyes; rather, a jurist is only someone who has understood the secret of being brought into existence and that He did not bring him into existence for any purpose other than to obey and serve Him. If he [truly] understands this latter point, then this understanding (*fiqh*) will be a cause for his abstinence from this world, his dedication to the Hereafter, his neglect of personal interests and occupying himself with his Master's rights, thinking about the final destination and preparing for it.

The Messenger of Allah ﷺ said, 'A strong believer is better according to Allah than a weak believer; and in each there is good.'[78] A strong believer is he in whose heart the light of certainty has shone. Allah ﷻ said, 'And those Foremost (in

78. Narrated by Muslim, Aḥmad and Ibn Mājah. The wording of Muslim is 'The strong believer is better and more beloved to Allah ﷻ'.

Faith) will be Foremost (in the Hereafter). Those are they who will be brought nigh [to Allah]; in gardens of bliss' [Qur'an 56:10–12]. They have outstripped [others] to Allah and divested their hearts from other than Him, so they were not impeded by obstacles nor distracted from Allah by [worldly] attachments.[79] Hence, they outstripped [others] to Allah, as there was nothing to hinder them. Slaves have only been hindered from outstripping by the intensity of their attachment to other than Allah. Whenever their hearts are on the verge of travelling to Allah ﷻ, they are pulled back by that attachment which is fixed to them, and so they retreat, returning back to it [i.e. their attachment] and devoting themselves to it. The proximity [to Allah] is forbidden for someone of this description and ruled out for someone of this quality.

The pure heart

Understand His words ﷻ, 'A day whereon neither wealth nor children will avail; save him who comes to Allah with a pure heart' [Qur'an 26:88–89]. A pure heart is that which is not attached to anything other than Allah ﷻ. Also, [understand] His words ﷻ, 'You have come to Us alone just as We have created you the first time, and you have left behind what We bestowed upon you' [Qur'an 6:94]. It is understood from [this verse] that you are unable to reach Allah or arrive to Him [i.e. gnosis of Him] unless you are isolated from other than Him. Moreover, [understand] His words ﷻ, 'Did He not find you an orphan and thus gave [you] shelter' [Qur'an 93:6]; it is understood from this that Allah does not provide you with shelter unless you are truly an orphan to everything other than Him. Then there are his words ﷺ, 'Verily, Allah is single (*witr*); and He loves the single,' meaning the heart that is not divided by its attachment

79. In another edition it reads 'creation (*khalā'iq*)' instead of 'attachments (*'alā'iq*)'.

to creation.[80] Therefore, these hearts were for Allah and through Allah. Due to this [state], they are the people of proximity [to Allah] (*ahl al-ḥaḍrah*), who have been addressed by pure favour; so how can they rely upon other than Him, while it is they who actually [experientially] behold the existence of His Oneness?

The people of Allah were through Allah, so Allah was sufficient for them

Shaykh Abū Ḥasan al-Shādhilī ☙ said, 'The state of beholding became too intense for me, so I asked Him to veil that from me, and I was told, "If you had asked Him what Mūsā (His Messenger whom He spoke to (*kalīm*)), ʿĪsā (His spirit) and Muhammad (His beloved and elect ﷺ) asked Him, then He would not have done that; but instead ask Him to strengthen you." So I asked Him and He strengthened me.'

The people of understanding took from Allah and relied upon Him and were therefore assisted by Him, so He sufficed them regarding their concerns and dispelled from them their anxieties. They were busied with what He commanded them [to perform] from having time to consider what He had guaranteed for them, out of their realisation that He does not entrust them to other than Himself and nor does He deprive them of His grace. Consequently, they found comfort and stood in the garden of submission and the delight of consigning [their affairs to Allah]; and due to this, Allah raised their rank and perfected their lights.

Beneficial knowledge

You should know – may Allah ﷻ have mercy on you – that whenever knowledge is reiterated in the Mighty Book or in the purified Sunnah, then it is solely intended as beneficial knowledge

---

80. Narrated by al-Bukhārī (6047), Muslim (2677) and others.

that is accompanied by awe (*khashyah*) and encompassed by fear. Allah ﷻ said, 'Those truly fear Allah, among His servants, who have knowledge' [Qur'an 35:28]. He here explained that knowledge accompanies fear; thus it is the scholars who fear Allah. Furthermore, [consider] His words ﷻ, 'Verily, those who were given knowledge before it' [Qur'an 17:107]; 'But those who are firmly grounded in knowledge' [Qur'an 4:162]; 'And say, "My Lord, increase me in knowledge"' [Qur'an 20:114]. Also, [see] the Prophet's words ﷺ, 'The scholars are the inheritors of the prophets.' That which is solely meant by knowledge in all of these instances is beneficial knowledge that subdues one's caprice and curbs the lower self. Such [an understanding] is necessarily certain because the speech of Allah ﷻ and His Messenger ﷺ is far exalted above being interpreted in any other way. Beneficial knowledge is that which assists one in acts of obedience, and engenders awe of Allah ﷻ and stopping at the limits ordained by Him ﷻ. This is the science of the gnosis of Allah ﷻ. But whoever gives free rein to himself in [respect to] unrestrictive usage of Divine Oneness (*tawḥīd*) and does not restrict himself to the ostensive facets of the Sacred Law (Shariah) has thereby been thrown into the sea of heresy (*zandaqah*).[81] The point, however, is for one to be supported by the reality (*ḥaqīqah*) and bound by the Sacred Law. Moreover, whoever attains realisation is neither unrestrained with the reality nor stationary with the ostensive ascription to the Sacred Law; but is justly balanced between them. To remain stationary at the apparent ascription is a form of associating partners with Allah (*shirk*); yet, letting one's reins free with the reality, without confining oneself to the Sacred

81. [SM] That is because he will end up rejecting the Sacred Law (Shariah) that has been conveyed by the Messenger ﷺ, which is pure heresy. Likewise, if he confines himself to the Sacred Law, he will fall prey to hidden polytheism (*shirk*), because he has not realised sincerity in the deeds of the Sacred Law. Actions are but standing images, and their soul is the presence of sincerity in them.

Law, is a repudiation (*ta'ṭīl*);[82] and so the station of guidance is that which is in between the two.

Every knowledge wherein thoughts [of other than Allah] precede to you, which are followed by images, and towards which the lower self inclines, and wherein one's nature takes delight, then discard it, even if it is true. Instead adhere to Allah's knowledge which He revealed to His Messenger ﷺ. Emulate him ﷺ, his successors (*khulafā'*) after him, the Companions and their followers after them, and those guides to Allah ﷻ, the Imams who have divested themselves of caprice. [By] following them, you will be safe from doubts and conjecture, illusions and misgivings, and false claims that lead one astray from guidance and its realities. It suffices you [to take] of beneficial knowledge the knowledge of Divine Oneness; and the knowledge (*'ilm*)[83] of the love of Allah, His Messenger ﷺ and his Companions, and believing that the truth is with the *Ahl al-Sunnah wa al-Jamā'ah*. If you want to have a portion of what Allah's friends ﷻ have, then you have to totally dismiss people [from your foremost affections], except for someone who guides you to Allah ﷻ. [Such a guide instructs you] either by way of true indication (*ishārah ṣādiqah*) or by established deeds that are not nullified by the Book and the Sunnah. Raise your aspiration to your Master and occupy yourself with Him and no one else.

I heard Shaykh Abū al-'Abbās al-Mursī ؓ say, 'By Allah, I have not seen honour except in raising one's aspirations from creation.' Remember – may Allah have mercy on you – His words ﷻ, 'But honour belongs to Allah and His Messenger, and

82. [SM] In other words, repudiation of legal responsibility for one to comply with the injunctions and prohibitions of the Sacred Law (*taklīf*). This is why Imam Mālik said, 'Whoever practises Sufism but does not study Islamic law (*fiqh*) will definitely become an heretic (*tazandaqa*); whereas someone who studies Islamic law but does not practise Sufism will definitely become morally corrupt (*tafassaqa*). However, whoever joins between the two will certainly attain realisation (*taḥaqqa*)'.

83. In the manuscript edition it reads '*amal* [actions]' instead of '*'ilm*'.

to the believers' [Qur'an 63:8]. Part of the distinction with which Allah has honoured the believer is that he raises his aspiration to his Master and [makes him] rely on Him and no one else.

Be shy before Allah, after He has clothed you in the garment of faith and adorned you with gnosis, that heedlessness and forgetfulness prevail over you until you end up inclining towards creation or seeking benevolence from other than Him.

It is disgraceful for a believer to present his need to other than his Master despite knowing His Oneness and His exclusivity in His Lordship, all the while he hears Allah's words ﷻ, 'Is not Allah sufficient for His servant' [Qur'an 39:36]. Let him also remember His words ﷻ, 'O you who believe, fulfil your contracts' [Qur'an 5:1]. Amongst the contracts which you have sealed with Him is that you will not raise your needs to anyone other than Him and that you will not rely upon anyone except Him. Raising one's aspirations from creation is the scale of [measuring one's] impoverishment: 'But establish the scales with justice' [Qur'an 55:9]. Thus, the truthful becomes manifest for his truthfulness, as does the [false] claimant for his lie.

Allah ﷻ has tested – with His wisdom and favour – the *fuqarā'* [Sufi pretenders] who are not genuine by exposing the base desire they conceal, so they expended themselves for worldly people, socialising with them, conforming to them in their ambitions, and being driven away from their doors. You see one of them adorn himself as does a bride. They are concerned with mending their exteriors, oblivious to mending their innermost beings. The Real has branded them in a way that disclosed their flaw and revealed their affairs. Initially, they were ascribed to Allah, and if they had been honest with Allah, then they would been called the slaves of the Great One (*al-Kabīr*); but now they have been divested of this ascription, so they are instead called the shaykhs of the governor (*al-amīr*).

The latter are the ones who falsely attribute [matters] to Allah, who dissuade the servants from accompanying Allah's friends, because what the laymen witness from them, they impute that to everyone who is associated with Allah, whether genuine or a pretender. Therefore, they are veils between the people of realisation, and the clouds between the sun of the people of divine enablement (*tawfīq*). They have beaten their drums, raised their flags, worn their armour, but when the attack is launched, they turn on their heels. Their tongues are unfastened in their claims, while their hearts are empty of God-consciousness! Have they not heard His words ﷻ, 'That He may question the truthful about their truthfulness' [Qur'an 33:8]? Do you think that He will leave the claimants without interrogation when He will interrogate the truthful about their truthfulness? Have they not heard His words ﷻ, 'And say [unto them], "Act! Allah will behold your actions, and [so will] His Messenger and the believers, and you will be brought back to the Knower of the Invisible and the Visible, and He will tell you what you used to do"' [Qur'an 9:105]? In their outward appearance they are merely pretending to be of the truthful, while their deeds are of those who have shunned [the right course]. Allah ﷻ said, 'Enter houses through their [proper] doors' [Qur'an 2:189].

The door to provision is open

Know that the door to provision is obedience to the Provider. So how can it be sought from Him through disobedience to Him? Moreover, how is it possible for His grace to descend when [one is] in opposition to Him? He ﷺ said, 'That which is with Allah cannot be gained by His displeasure';[84] namely, His provisions

84. Al-Ḥākim narrated it with similar wording and graded it as rigorously authentic, and al-Dhahabī agreed with him; the wording is, 'There is no deed that brings one close to Paradise except I have commanded you with it... So if one of you finds that his provision is slow [in being acquired], then let him not seek it through disobedience to Allah ﷻ, for verily Allah's bounty is not attained through disobedience to Him.'

are not sought except through [deeds that gain] His pleasure. He ﷻ explained this further with His words, 'And for whoever fears Allah, He [ever] prepares a way out, and He provides for him from [sources] he could never imagine' [Qur'an 65:2–3]. Due to this meaning, when Shaykh Abū al-'Abbās ؓ, said in his litany, 'And give us such and such,' [he went on to] ask, 'and [give us] agreeable, trouble-free provisions wherein there is no veil in this world, nor for which there is accountability, interrogation or punishment in the Hereafter.' Such people are therefore on the rug of the knowledge of *tawḥīd* [Allah's Oneness] and the Sacred Law, free from caprice, base desire and avarice.

Relinquishment of planning alongside Allah ﷻ

Beware of planning your affairs alongside Allah ﷻ! The similitude of someone who plans his affairs alongside Allah is like that of a slave who has been sent by his master to a city to produce for him some garments. Then, upon entering that city, the slave began saying to himself, 'Where shall I live, and whom shall I marry?' He subsequently became occupied with that and dedicated himself to these pursuits, neglecting his master's command until eventually he summoned him. Consequently, his recompense from his master was that he dismissed him and denied him access to him; [this is all] because his preoccupation with his own pursuits [prevented him] from tending to his master's rights. Likewise is the case with you, O believer, [because] the Real brought you out to this abode and commanded you to serve Him therein, while He undertook planning your affairs for you out of His benevolence. Therefore, if you are preoccupied therein with planning for your own affairs from tending to your Master's right, then you have strayed from the path of guidance and [instead] trodden on the paths to destruction.

The similitude of one who plans [his affairs] alongside Allah and the one who does not is like that of two slaves who belong to a king: as for one of them, he is busy with his master's orders, inattentive to [his own] clothing or food; rather, his concern is serving the master to the exclusion of tending to his personal interests. As for the other slave, then whenever his master summons him, he finds him washing his own clothes, training his own mount and grooming himself! So the first slave is more deserving of his master's attention than the second slave. A slave is only purchased for his master, not for himself. Similarly, you will not see an insightful, successful slave except that he is busy with Allah's rights, complying with His orders and abstaining from His prohibitions, and [restraining himself] from pursuing his own personal desires and interests. Accordingly, the Real ﷻ took care of all his affairs and turned to him with abundant gifts, due to the genuineness of his reliance [on Him]; as in His words ﷻ, 'Whoever relies upon Allah, then He suffices him' [Qur'an 65:3]. The heedless person on the other hand is the opposite: you will not find him except that he is busy attaining his worldly pursuits and whatever satisfies his whim.

The similitude of a slave with Allah in this abode is like that of a child with his mother: his mother is not one to neglect planning [the welfare] for her child in her custody and deprive him of her care. Likewise a believer is with Allah: He takes care of him through good custody, delivers to him His favours and wards tribulations off him.

The similitude of a slave in this world is like that of a slave whose master says to him, 'Go to such and such a land, then prepare well to travel from it to such and such uncultivated land, and take what you need.' If his master permitted him that, then it is obvious that he has allowed him to eat that which will assist him in maintaining himself so that he may strive in undertaking all preparations. A slave is in a similar case with Allah: He brought him into existence in this abode and commanded him to take provisions from it for his return. He ﷻ said, 'And make provision, for verily the best provision is God-consciousness'

[Qur'an 2:197]. It is obvious that when He commands him to make provision for the Hereafter, He will permit him to take from this world that which will assist him in making provision for the Hereafter and preparing him for his return.

The similitude of a slave with Allah is like that of an employee whom the king brings to his villa and orders him to do a task for him. Now the king is not one to bring in an employee, employ him in his house and leave him without feeding him, as he is more generous than that. Likewise is the case of the slave with Allah: this world is Allah's villa, the employee is you, the task is obedience and the wage is Paradise; and Allah is not one to command you to do a job without giving you that which will assist you therein.

Moreover, the similitude of a slave with Allah ﷻ is like that of a slave whose master commands him to stay in a land and to fight and struggle against the enemy therein. It is obvious that when he has commanded him to do that, he has allowed him to faithfully eat from the treasuries of that land in order for it to assist him in fighting the enemy. Likewise is the case with the slaves [of Allah]: the Real ﷻ has commanded them to fight and struggle against their lower selves and Satan; as in His words ﷻ, 'And faithfully struggle for the sake of Allah; He has chosen you' [Qur'an 22:78], and, 'Verily, Satan is an enemy to you, so take him as an enemy' [Qur'an 35:6]. Since He has ordered the slave to fight him, He has permitted him to take from the produce of His land that which will assist him in fighting Satan, for if you had gone without food and drink, you would not have been able to obey Him, nor to earnestly serve Him.

In addition, the similitude of a slave with Allah is like that of a king who has slaves; he builds a house, decorates and embellishes it, takes care in planting its trees, and completes it with fanciful things therein. [This house] is not the dwelling of the slaves; but [all along] he intends to transfer them to it. Tell me, if this is his concern for them with regard to what he has stored away for them with himself and prepared for them after their journey, will he prevent them from now partaking in his bounties and his surplus food, whilst he has prepared for them a tremendous affair and an immense favour? Likewise is the case of the slaves with Allah: He has put them in this world and prepared Paradise for them, but He does not want to stop them from partaking from this world, though only to the extent that will keep them alive. He ﷻ said, 'Eat of the good things and work righteousness' [Qur'an 23:51], and, 'O you who believe, eat of the good things which We have provided you' [Qur'an 2:172]. If He has stored away for you that which is everlasting and has favoured you with it, then He will not deprive you of the transitory. He will merely deprive you of that which He has not apportioned for you, and that which He has not apportioned for you is not yours.

The similitude of someone who is worried about his worldly affairs, yet heedless of gathering provision for his Hereafter, is like that of a person whom a predatory animal suddenly attacks by surprise and seeks to devour but then a fly falls on him and he becomes preoccupied with repelling and warding off the fly, rather than guarding himself against the predatory animal. The truth of the matter is that this is a foolish, unintelligent slave; if he had intelligence, he would have been busy [guarding himself] from the lion, and its pouncing and attacking him, as opposed to being concerned about the fly. Likewise is the case of the person who is distracted by his worldly affairs from paying attention to gathering provisions for the Hereafter. Such behaviour demonstrates his stupidity, because if he was astute and intelligent, he would have prepared for the Hereafter, which is his responsibility and for which he will be called to account. Therefore, he should not be occupied with his provisions, because concern for it in relation to the Hereafter is like that of the fly in relation to the lion's sudden appearance and attack.

Whoever stores away possessions entrusted to him is like a king's slave who does not consider himself to possess anything alongside his master, nor does he rely upon storing away that which is in his hands, nor does he have an alternative and nor does he choose except what his master chooses for him. If this slave understands that withholding [what he is entrusted with] is his master's desire, then he withholds it for his master's sake, not for himself, until he discovers the cause upon which it is best spent, so that he spends it when he understands that his master wants it to be spent [in that manner]. Such a person is not to be blamed for his withholding, because he has withheld for his master's sake, not for himself. The people who have gnosis of Allah are similar to this: if they spend, they do so for His sake; and if they withhold, they do so for Him; they seek to satisfy Him, and they do not seek in their spending or withholding other than Him. Thus, they are trustworthy treasurers, esteemed slaves, and noble, righteous people. The Real had liberated them from the enslavement to creation (*āthār*),[85] so they did not incline to it with love, nor attend to it with fondness. They were prevented from that by the love and fondness for Allah which He placed in their hearts and by His grandeur and majesty which filled their chests. So things in their hands became as if they were in Allah's treasuries before having reached them, due to their knowledge that both they and that which Allah ﷻ has bestowed upon them belong to Him.

An exposition for those who benefit from admonishment and seek insight

The following is an exposition for those who benefit from admonishment and a guidance for those seeking insight. Whoever relinquishes planning for himself, then Allah will take it upon Himself to plan beautifully for him.

85. *Āthār* literally means 'manifestations' (i.e. of His power).

Planning is of two types: praiseworthy and blameworthy.

The blameworthy type is any planning that revolves around your self because of its gratification, and wherein there is nothing for Allah. For example, using one's intelligence[86] to plan the performance of an act of disobedience, or purely for [the fulfilment of] self-gratification, or [performing] an act of obedience with ostentation, self-promotion and the like. All of this is blameworthy because it either entails punishment [in the Hereafter] or it necessitates one being veiled [from the gnosis of Allah].

Whoever realises the blessing of the intellect is ashamed before Allah ﷻ for expending his intellect in planning for that which does not bring him closer to Him, or that which is not a means for attaining His love. The intellect is the greatest favour that Allah has bestowed upon His slaves. That is because He ﷻ created everything that exists and graced them by bringing them into existence and continually sustaining them, and so all existent things shared in the fact that He had brought them into existence and sustained them. The Real ﷻ, however, wanted to distinguish man over them and so He granted him intellect and strengthened him by virtue of it, and thereby made him superior to the animals and perfected His favour upon mankind. By virtue of the intellect, and its expansiveness, illumination and light, the interests of this world and the Hereafter are fulfilled. To therefore expend the blessing of the intellect in planning for this world, which is worthless in Allah's sight ﷻ, is a rejection of the blessing of the intellect. In contrast, directing it to prioritise putting right his state for his Afterlife, showing gratitude towards the One who is benevolent towards him and who floods him with His light, is more worthy, more fitting, better and more appropriate for him. Do not therefore expend your intellect, with which Allah has favoured you, in planning for this world, which

86. In another printed edition it reads 'because of obliviousness'.

is just as the Messenger of Allah ﷺ described in his words 'This world is a filthy carcass'; and just as he said to Ḍaḥḥāk, 'What is your food?' He replied, 'Meat and milk.' So he said, 'Then where do they end up?' He replied, 'To where you well know, O Messenger of Allah.' He said, 'Verily, Allah has made that which exits out from man [literally, the son of Ādam] a similitude for this world.'[87]

Praiseworthy planning is that which brings you closer to Allah ﷻ, such as planning on how to fulfil the rights that one owes people, either through discharging them or seeking absolution and pardon, or correcting one's repentance to the Lord of the Worlds, or reflecting about that which will lead to suppressing one's destructive caprice and the misleading Satan. All of this is undoubtedly praiseworthy, which is why the Messenger of Allah ﷺ said, 'Reflection for a moment is better than worshipping for seventy years.'[88]

Planning for this world is of two types: planning for this world for the sake of this world, and planning for this world for the sake of the Hereafter.

Planning for this world for the sake of this world is to plan the means for amassing it out of pride in it and seeking more of it. Now the more one gains of it, the more one becomes heedless and deluded. The sign of this [state] is that it preoccupies him from obedience [to Allah] and leads him to disobedience.

---

87. Imam Aḥmad narrated on the authority of al-Ḍaḥḥāk ibn Sufyān al-Kilābī that the Messenger of Allah ﷺ said to him, 'O Ḍaḥḥāk, what is your food?' He replied, 'O Messenger of Allah, meat and milk.' So he replied, 'Then what becomes of it?' He replied, 'To that which you know.' He replied, 'Verily, Allah ﷻ has made that which exits out from man [literally, the son of Ādam] a similitude for this world.'

88. [SM] Al-'Irāqī says in *al-Mughnī 'an ḥaml al-asfār*, 'Ibn Ḥibbān narrated with his chain of transmission in the Book of 'Aẓamah the hadith of Abū Hurayrah with the wording "sixty years" with a weak chain of transmission'; and a weak chain is acceptable in virtuous acts (*al-faḍā'il*).

Planning for this world for the sake of the Hereafter is like someone who manages his business so that he may consume from it the lawful, or that he may spend on the needy out of kindness and to generally save face with people [by not asking]. The sign of such [a state] is to not amass and store away [wealth], and to assist others and prefer them over oneself.

It is thus clear from the above that not every seeker of this world is to be blamed; rather, the one who is to be condemned is he who seeks it for himself, not for his Lord, and [seeks it] for his worldly benefit, not for his Hereafter. People therefore are of two types: a slave who seeks this world for the sake of this world, and a slave who seeks this world for the sake of the Hereafter.

The gnostic has neither this world nor the Hereafter

I heard our Shaykh Abū al-'Abbās al-Mursī ﷺ say, 'The gnostic has neither this world nor the Hereafter, because this world of his is for his Hereafter, and his Hereafter is for his Lord.' The states of the Companions [of the Prophet ﷺ] and the early righteous Muslim community ﷺ are to be understood in light of this. Whenever they engaged with worldly activities, they did so in order to thereby draw near to Allah and to ascribe to His good pleasure. They did not thereby seek this world and its ornament and delights. Consequently, the Real ﷻ described them with His words, 'Muhammad is the Messenger of Allah, and those with him are stern against the disbelievers, merciful between themselves; you see them bowing and prostrating, seeking bounty from Allah and [His] pleasure' [Qur'an 48:29].

What do you think about a people whom Allah loves and has chosen for the companionship of His Messenger ﷺ and for them to be directly addressed in His revelation? There is not a single believer till the Day of Resurrection except that he is indebted to the Companions due to their countless acts of benevolence and unforgettable favours, for they are the ones who transmitted wisdom and laws to us from the Prophet ﷺ, clarified the lawful from the unlawful, understood the particular and general [purport of rulings], conquered regions and countries, and subdued the idolaters and the defiant. Therefore, his words ﷺ 'My Companions are like stars: whichever of them you follow, you will be guided'[89] aptly applies to them. Allah has described their qualities in a noble verse; He says, 'They

---

89. [SM] This hadith is not authentic (*ṣaḥīḥ*) according to the scholars, but they have differed as to whether it is fabricated (*mawḍū'*), very weak or merely weak (*ḍa'īf*) in respect to some of its chains of transmission, and a weak hadith is accepted by the scholars in *faḍā'il*, especially when there are supporting hadiths. Al-Ḥāfiẓ Abū Bakr al-Bayhaqī said in his book *al-I'tiqād*, after mentioning the hadith of Abū Mūsā, which he ascribed back to the Prophet ﷺ, that 'The stars are [a source of] safety for the skies; when the stars disappear, then what the inhabitants of the skies have been threatened with will befall them. My Companions are a safety for my nation, and when my Companions disappear, then what my nation has been threatened with will transpire'. Muslim narrated it with the same meaning. It has been narrated in an uninterrupted hadith (*mawṣūl*) with a weak chain of transmission, and in another interrupted chain of transmission (*munqaṭi'*), that he ﷺ said, 'The similitude of my Companions is like the similitude of the stars in the skies; whoever adopts one of the stars, he will be guided.' He said, 'The rigorously authentic hadith which we have narrated here conveys its meaning partially.' Sirāj al-Dīn ibn Mulaqqin, *al-Badr al-munīr fī takhrīj al-aḥādīth wa al-āthār al-wāqi'ah fī al-sharḥ al-Kabīr* (n.p.), 9:587.

Ibn Ḥajar says in *Talkhīṣ al-Ḥabīr*, 'Bayhaqī was right in that it conveys the validity of comparing the Companions to the stars specifically; as for emulating them, it is not obvious in the hadith of Abū Mūsā. Yes, it is possible to infer that from the meaning of seeking guidance from the stars. The apparent meaning of the hadith is only an indication to the tribulations that will occur after the end of the epoch of the Companions, such as the disappearance of the Prophetic practices (*sunan*), the prevalence of innovations and the widespread immorality across the globe. Allah is sought for help.' *Ibid.* 5:498. 'Umar ibn 'Abd al-'Azīz understood from this hadith that their difference of opinion is a [source of] mercy; he said, 'I would not have been happy if the Messenger of Allah's Companions did not differ with one another [on legal rulings], because if they did not have any differences of opinion, then there would not have been any dispensations (*rukhṣah*).' Ibn Baṭṭah, *al-Ibānah al-kubrā* (n.p.), 2:221.

seek bounty from Allah and [His] good pleasure' [Qur'an 59:8]. His words ﷻ prove that they did not seek and intend with the worldly possessions they bore other than His noble countenance and tremendous bounty. He ﷻ said in another verse, 'In houses which Allah has permitted to be exalted and for His name to be mentioned therein; in them He is glorified in the mornings and in the evenings. [Those are] men whom neither merchandise nor selling diverts them from the remembrance of Allah' [Qur'an 24:36–37]. He did not negate from them [the engagement with] worldly means, business or buying and selling, so their wealth does not disqualify them from [His] praise when they fulfilled their Master's rights.

This world is in their hands, not in their hearts

'Abd-Allāh ibn 'Utbah said, 'On the day that he was murdered, 'Uthmān ibn 'Affān[90] ﷺ had 100,500 gold dinars and 1,000,000

Al-Munāwī says in *Fayḍ al-Qadīr*, 'Al-Ḥakīm al-Tirmidhī says regarding the hadith "My Companions are like the stars: whichever of them you follow", "Not everyone who met him and followed him or only saw him once is included in it; but rather [it refers to] those who adhered to him morning and evening and thus would receive revelation and take the Sacred Law from him, which was prescribed as a methodology for the nation; and [the ones who would] look into the etiquette of Islam and its qualities, so they became after him Imams, guides and exemplars to be followed, and through them is safety and faith."' Ibn 'Abd al-Barr said in his explanation, 'It is as has been explained by al-Muzanī and others from amongst the people of erudition that it [being guided by them] is regarding the transmission [of Prophetic hadiths], because all of them are reliable, trustworthy and upright ﷺ; therefore, it is necessary to accept what anyone of them has transmitted and testified to the Prophet ﷺ.'

90. He was the third rightly guided caliph and the Prophet's son-in-law ﷺ, having married two of his daughters, Ruqayyah and Umm Kulthūm ﷺ, one after another, which is why he was called Dhū Nūrayn (the Possessor of the Two Lights) ﷺ. He was martyred by some rebels in 35 AH at the age of eighty-two.

silver dirhams, and he left behind 1,000 horses, 1,000 slaves and [the following] real estate: the Wells of 'Arīs, Khaybar and Wādī al-Qurā, whose value was 200,000 dinars.' 'Amr ibn al-'Āṣ[91] left behind 300,000 dinars. The wealth of Zubayr ibn al-'Awwām[92] reached 50,000 dinars, and he had left behind 1,000 horses and 1,000 slaves. The wealth of 'Abd al-Raḥmān ibn al-'Awf ﷺ[93] is too well known to be mentioned.

This world was in their hands, not in their hearts. They were patient when they lacked it, and grateful to Allah when they had it. Allah only tried them with poverty and need in the beginning of their affair until [eventually] their lights were perfected and their innermost beings were purified; thereupon, He lavished it upon them generously. Had they been given it before that, it may have captivated them. But when they were given it after fortitude and a deep-rooted certainty, they spent it like a faithful

91. 'Amr ibn al-'Āṣ accepted Islam in the eighth year after Hegira when he was more than fifty years of age. The Prophet ﷺ would keep him close to himself due to his bravery and knowledge and put him in charge of the Dhat al-Salāsil expedition; he later appointed him as governor over Oman. 'Umar, during his reign, appointed him at the head of the army that would successfully conquer Egypt. He was thereafter appointed as 'Umar's governor in Egypt, where he passed away in 43 AH at the age of ninety-four.

92. Zubayr ibn al-'Awwām is the Prophet's paternal cousin ﷺ and one of the ten to be given the glad tidings of Paradise by him. He was also one of the six-man consultative team appointed by 'Umar to select the caliph to succeed him ﷺ. Zubayr was the first to unleash the sword in Allah's way. He participated in all of the Prophet's military expeditions ﷺ. He was martyred in 36 AH.

93. 'Abd al-Raḥmān ibn al-'Awf is also one of the ten to be given the glad tidings of Paradise by the Prophet ﷺ and one of the six-man consultative team appointed by 'Umar to select the caliph to succeed him ﷺ. He migrated both to Abysinnia, when the Muslims were persecuted in Mecca, and then to Medina with the Prophet ﷺ. He was one of the few who stood their ground with the Prophet ﷺ on the battleground of Uḥud, when others fled. He passed away in 31 AH at the age of seventy-five in Medina, and was buried in Baqī'. 'Uthmān led his funeral prayer in accordance with his bequest.

treasurer, and they complied therein with the words of the Lord of the Worlds, 'And spend of that whereof He has made you trustees' [Qur'an 57:7]. And so this world was in the hands of the Companions, not in their hearts.

It suffices you to know that 'Umar ibn al-Khaṭṭāb ﷺ[94] expended half of his wealth, Abū Bakr al-Ṣiddīq ﷺ[95] expended all of his wealth, 'Abd al-Raḥmān ibn al-'Awf ﷺ financed 700 camels laden with supplies, 'Uthmān ibn al-'Affān ﷺ [financially] prepared the Army of Difficulty (*Jaysh al-'Usrah*), and other examples of their beautiful deeds and elevated states, may Allah forever be pleased with them all. The foregoing verses contain an endorsement of their external and internal states, and affirm their praiseworthy and glorious virtues.

It has become clear from the foregoing that planning is of two types: planning for this world for the sake of this world, as is the state of those ignoble, heedless people who have severed their ties with Allah; and planning for this world for the sake of the Hereafter, as is the case of the noblest Companions and the righteous predecessors, may Allah be well pleased with them all and make us amongst those who follow them. *Āmīn*; rather, a million *āmīns*!

---

94. He is the second rightly guided caliph, the first caliph to be given the title 'the Leader of the Believers' and the Prophet's father-in-law ﷺ. He ﷺ gave him the epithet *al-Fārūq*, which means the criterion, because by virtue of him the truth was distinguished from falsehood. He was martyred at the hand of a Magian servant called Abū Lu'lu'ah in 23 AH at the age of sixty-three.

95. He was the first rightly guided caliph to succeed the Prophet ﷺ, his father-in-law and companion on his migration to Medina. He is considered to be the best Companion according to Sunni orthodoxy and there are copious narrations demonstrating his rank and virtue. The Prophet ﷺ said, 'The sun has neither risen nor set over anyone better than Abū Bakr, after the prophets and the messengers.' He passed away in 13 AH at the age of sixty-three and was buried in 'Ā'ishah's room, next to the Prophet ﷺ.

***The hidden voices of realities* (hawātif)**[96]

We shall mention herein the Real's private discourse ﷻ with His slave on the tongues of the hidden voices of realities regarding [the subject of] planning and provision.

O slave, listen attentively as you behold! More shall come to you from Me, and pay attention, for I am not remote from you. You were in My planning for you before you were for your self, so be for your self by not being for it. I took care of it [i.e. your self] before your emergence, and I am now still taking care of it.

I am alone in creating and fashioning, and I am alone in decreeing and planning. You did not participate with Me in My creating and fashioning, so do not participate with Me in My decreeing and planning.

I am the One who plans for My dominion and I do not have an assistant therein; and I am alone in decreeing and thus not in need of a vizier.

O slave, [regarding] the One who was planning for you before bringing you into existence, do not compete with Him in what He Wills; and [regarding] the One who accustomed you to His beautiful care for you, do not confront Him with defiance.

I accustomed you to My excellent care for you, so accustom Me to your relinquishing planning alongside [My planning].

Is there any doubt after experience, confusion after exposition or deviation after clear guidance? You have submitted to Me in My management of My kingdom, and you are from My kingdom, so do not dispute with Me about My Lordship and do not oppose [Me] by your planning alongside My Divinity.

---

96. [SM] These are inspirations (*wāridāt*) that Allah brings on the tongues of created things around him, so he hears from them as if they are from the Real, and they penetrate the heart of a slave in a manner that he understands in it from Allah what He wants from him by way of these created things addressing him.

When have I made you in need of yourself, such that you assign your affairs to yourself?

When have I entrusted anything of My kingdom to anyone else, such that I would entrust any of it to you?

When has the one whose affairs I was planning been disappointed? And when has the one to whom I was a support been forsaken?

O slave, let your service to Me preoccupy you from seeking what I apportion [for you], and let your good opinion of Me stop you from suspecting My Lordship. It is not befitting to suspect a benevolent one, nor to dispute with a powerful one, nor for an overpowering one to be opposed, nor for a wise one to be objected to, nor for one to be worried when with someone kind.

Whoever has divested himself from his will [in order to place reliance] with Me has truly succeeded. Whoever transfers his affairs to Me has been guided to the facilitation of his affairs. Whenever a slave moves through Me alone, then he has truly made himself entitled to triumph by Me. Whoever holds firmly to My rope has truly held on to the strongest rope.

O slave, We want you to want Us and not for you to want [someone else] alongside Us. We want you to choose Us and not to choose [someone else] alongside Us. We are pleased for you to be pleased with Us and not to be pleased with other than Us. Just as you have submitted to Me [in] My planning on My earth and heaven, and My exclusive judgement and decree in them, then hand over your existence to Me, for verily you belong to Me. Do not plan alongside Me, for verily you are with Me. Take Me as an agent and trust Me as a guarantor, and I shall give you abundantly and gift you tremendous glory.

Woe to you! We have deemed your status to be much loftier than for Us to employ you for your own affair, so do not belittle your status.

O the one whom We have elevated, do not abase yourself by transferring your affairs to other than Us.

O the one whom We have honoured, woe to you! You are far too great in Our sight for Us to employ you for other than Us.

For My proximity I have created you; to it I have addressed you; and by the gravitational pull of My care to it I have pulled you. So if you occupy yourself with your self, I will veil you; and if you follow its caprice, I will expel you; and if you divest yourself of it, I will bring you near; and if you show Me love, by turning away from other than Me, I shall love you.

O slave, whoever disputes Me has not believed in Me, and whoever plans alongside Me has not realised My Oneness. Furthermore, whoever complains to other than Me about what I have afflicted him with is not satisfied with Me. Moreover, whoever has chosen alongside Me has not chosen Me, and whoever did not submit to My compelling force has not complied with My command.

If you were to seek to plan, then you would be ignorant; so what about when you [actually] plan for it? If you had chosen alongside Me, you would not have been just; so what about when you choose [someone] over Me?

O the one who is worried about his self, if you had cast it to Us, then you could have relaxed.

Woe to you! The burdens of planning cannot be borne except by Lordship. Human weakness is unable to bear it.

Woe to you! You are carried, so do not [try to] be the carrier. We wanted you to be at ease, so do not tire yourself out.

O slave, I commanded you to serve Me, and guaranteed you My apportionment (*qismah*). But you have neglected what I commanded and doubted in what I guaranteed. I did not suffice Myself by merely guaranteeing until I swore an oath; and I did not suffice Myself in swearing an oath until I drew a similitude, so I addressed slaves who could understand and said, 'And in the heaven is your sustenance, as is also that which you are promised. Then by the Lord of the heavens and the earth! It is most surely the truth, just as you do speak' [Qur'an 51:22–23]. I have given provisions to the one who was heedless of Me and disobeyed Me, so how can I not provide for someone who obeys Me and calls on Me?

Woe to you! The one who really plants a tree is the one who waters it, and the One who sustains creation is the One who has originated it. From Me was the bringing forth of existence, and upon Me is [the duty] to continually sustain it. From Me was creation and upon Me is [the duty] to continually provide for it. Do I allow you to enter My abode yet deprive you of My kindness? Do I bring you forth to My creation yet deprive you of My assistance? Do I bring you forth to My existence (*wujūdī*) yet deprive you of My generosity (*jūdī*)?

For you I have prepared My grace, and in you I have manifested My mercy. I was not satisfied for you to have this world until I stored away for you My Garden; and I did not suffice Myself [with giving the Garden] to you so I gifted you the vision of Me.

If My actions are [as you know them], then how can you doubt My benevolence? Therefore, choose Me and do not choose [others] over Me, and genuinely turn your heart to Me. If you do so, I will show you the wonders of My benevolence and My unparalleled generosity, and give delight to your innermost being (*sirr*) by beholding Me.

I have made manifest the path to those accomplished, and have made clear the landmarks of guidance for those given divine enablement. So it is right that those with certainty have submitted to Me, and the believers have put their trust in Me due to [My] exposition. They knew that I am better to them than they are to themselves, and that My planning [their affairs] for them is more fitting than their planning for themselves, so they submitted fully to My Lordship, and cast themselves before Me in resignation. Therefore, I compensated them for that [by placing] comfort in their souls, a light in their intellects, gnosis in their hearts and realisation of My proximity in their innermost beings. This is in this abode; and I have prepared to magnify their status and elevate their position when they arrive to Me; and they have, when I allow them to enter My abode, that which no eye has seen, no ear has heard and no human has imagined.

O slave, I have not demanded from you service [to Me] in the time that awaits you [in the future], so do not demand from Me therein apportionment [of provisions]. When I charge you, I take responsibility for you, and when I employ you, I feed you.

Know that I do not forget you, even if you forget Me, and that I have enabled your remembrance before you ever remembered Me; and that My sustaining you is perpetual, even if you disobey Me. If you are apathetic to Me, [and I treat you so generously,] then how do you think I will be when you devote [yourself] to Me? You have underestimated Me if you do not submit to My omnipotence, and have not truly considered My goodness if you do not comply with My command. Do not shun Me, for you shall not find a substitute for Me, and do not be deceived by others, for none shall be of any avail to you against Me.

I am the One who created you with My power, and I am the One who generously bestows my grace upon you. Just as there is no creator other than Me, likewise there is no provider other than Me. Do I create and transfer [people's needs] to others when I am the Benevolent, and deprive My slaves of My goodness when I am the Beneficent?

Therefore, O slave, trust in Me, for I am the Lord of the slaves, and leave your desire so that I deliver you to the true goal. In addition, remember My preceding kindness and do not forget the right of mutual love.

The author's intimate discourses (**munājāt**) ≈ *with his Lord*

My God, I am impoverished in my affluence, so how can I not be impoverished in my poverty? I am ignorant in my knowledge, so how can I not be ignorant in my ignorance?

My God, from me is that which befits my callousness, and from You is that which befits Your generosity. If virtuous deeds and traits emanate from me, then it is out of Your grace, and I am beholden to You. If offences and blameworthy traits emanate from me, then it is out of Your justice; and You have a proof against me.

My God, how can You leave me to my own devices when You have made me rely on you? How could I be treated unjustly when You are my succor? How can I be disappointed when You are the One gracious to me?

Here I am seeking proximity to You by means (*tawassul*) of my impoverishment. How can I ask You by means of something that cannot possibly reach You? How can I complain to You about my condition when it is not hidden from You? How can I express the words [in my heart] when it is from You that they emerge,[97] and to You [their affair returns]? How can my hopes be unfulfilled when they have arrived to You? How can my states not be improved when they have subsisted through You and to You [their affair returns]?

My God, how kind You are to me despite my ignorance; and how merciful You are to me despite my abominable deeds! How close You are to me, yet how remote I am from You; and how compassionate You are to me! So what is it that veils me from You?

My God, just as my callousness has made me mute, so too Your generosity has made me speak. Whenever my qualities make me despair, Your grace makes me optimistic.

My God, whosoever's virtuous deeds are [in reality] faults, then how can his faults not be faults? And whosoever's realities are claims, then how can his claims not be claims?

My God, how can I have resolve when You are the Dominator, and how can I not resolve when You are the One who gives orders?

97. Namely, He gave him the ability to speak.

My frequenting creation necessitates remoteness from the arrival [to You],[98] so allow me to devote myself to You through service that delivers me to You.

How can something which in its existence is contingent upon You be used as a proof for Your existence? Is there anything else that is more manifest than You such that it reveals You?

When were You absent such that You require a proof to guide to You, and when have You been remote such that creation directs unto You?

My God, the eye that does not see You as a guardian over it is blind, and the contract of a slave for whom You did not ordain a portion of Your love is a loss.[99]

My God, my humiliation is manifest before You, and my state is not hidden from You. From You I seek arrival and through You I am guided to You, so guide me by Your light to You,[100] and establish me in complete servitude to You.

My God, teach me from Your concealed knowledge,[101] protect me by the secret of Your protected name, make me realise the realities of the people of proximity, guide me along the paths of the people of *jadhb* [divine selection],[102] suffice me from having to plan for myself by planning for me and [suffice me] with Your choosing from me having to choose for myself, station me at the

98. 'This is beholding His Oneness and perfection through gnosis.' Ibn 'Abbād, *Sharḥ al-Ḥikam*, 541.

99. '"Love" here refers to His mercy, praise and generosity.' *Ibid.* 543.

100. 'The "light" here refers to the light of faith and certainty.' *Ibid.* 546.

101. 'In other words, the knowledge stored away with Him (*ladunī*), which is reserved for His elect friends.' *Ibid.* 541.

102. '*Ahl al-jadhb*, literally, the people of attraction, are those beloved to Him and selected by Him, who find no fatigue or hardship in their acts of worship, but instead find pleasure and delight, and that is because He has released them from the captivation of their lower selves.' *Ibid.* 547.

settlements of my helplessness, bring me out of the humiliation of my lower self, and purify me from my doubts and associating partners with You (*shirk*)[103] before the befalling of my death.

Through You I seek triumph, so grant me triumph. Upon You I place my trust, so do not forsake me. You alone I ask, so do not deprive me. Of Your grace I am desirous, so do not fail me. To Your entity I ascribe [myself], so do not turn me away. At Your door I stand, so do not expel me.

My God, verily divine destiny (*qaḍā' wa qadar*) has overwhelmed me, and caprice, with the shackles of base desire, has captured me. So be my support until You grant me triumph and insight, and suffice me with Your grace so that I am content with Your bounty from having to ask.

You are the One who has shone the lights in the hearts of Your friends, and You are the One who has removed the distractions from the innermost beings of Your loved ones. You are their comforter when they are alienated by the words, and You are the One who has guided them until the landmarks became clear to them.

What has one gained if he has lost You? And what has one lost if he has found You?

Whoever is satisfied with other than You as a substitute has truly failed, and whoever resorts to other than You to manage his affairs has truly lost.

How can one have hope in other than You when You have not ceased Your kindness? How can one seek from other than You when You have not changed Your custom of generosity?

O the One who has made His loved ones taste the sweetness of His intimate company, so they stood before Him courteously gaining His favour. O the One who has clothed His friends in the

103. 'Namely, the hidden *shirk,* which is for one to be attached to worldly means (*asbāb*) and obliviousness to the Creator of means (*musabbib*).' *Ibid.* 548.

garments of His awe, so they stood honoured by His might. You are the One who enables remembrance before [the existence of] those who remember, and You are the One who initiates with kindness before the worshippers devote themselves to You. You are the One who gives generously before those seeking can ask. You are the Benevolent and the One who has graced us with gifts, [and I am simply] the borrower, so seek me by Your mercy so that I may reach You, and draw me to Yourself by Your favour so that I may devote myself to You.

My God, my hope in You will never cease, even if I disobey You, just as my fear does not depart from me whilst I obey You. The worlds have pushed me towards You, and my knowledge of Your generosity has made me stand before You, so how can I fail when You are my hope, or how can I be subjected to humiliation when my reliance is upon You? How can I be honoured when You have embedded me in humiliation, or how can I not be honoured when You have ascribed me to Yourself? How can I not be impoverished when it is You who has established me in poverty, or how can I be impoverished when it is You who has enriched me by Your generosity?

You are the One besides whom there is no other god. You have made Yourself known to everything, so nothing is ignorant of You,[104] and You have made Yourself known to me in everything, so I have seen You manifest in everything;[105] for You are the One Manifest to everything.

---

104. 'In other words, He made Himself manifest to everything until it knew Him and glorified Him, as He ﷻ said, "And there is not a single thing but it glorifies Him with His praise, but you do not understand their glorification" [Qur'an 17:44].' al-Shurnūbī, *Sharḥ al-Ḥikam,* 82–83.

105. 'In other words, all things are manifestations of the meanings denoted by His names. Thus, the meaning of Him being *al-Muʿizz* [the One who bestows honour] appears in the people who are honoured, and the meaning of Him being *al-Mudhill* [the One who debases] appears in the people who are humiliated, and so forth.' *Ibid.* 82.

O the One whose all-mercifulness prevailed over His throne whereby the throne became concealed in His all-mercifulness, just as the worlds have become concealed in His throne. The creation (*āthār*) [i.e. the worlds] has been obliterated by the manifestation (*āthār*) [i.e. His throne], and You have erased the *aghyār*[106] by the surrounding celestial bodies of lights.[107]

O the One who has veiled Himself in the canopies of His might so that sight [does not] encompass Him. O the One who has manifested with the perfection of His splendour so that the innermost beings (*asrār*) have realised His grandeur. How can You be hidden when You are the Manifest (*Ẓāhir*),[108] or how can You be absent when You are the Guardian Present?

---

106. *Aghyār* literally means 'others' but in this context it means the throne.

107. In other words, Your mercy which resembles the celestial bodies that encompass the throne.

108. The author says in *al-Ḥikam*, 'All of the universe (*kawn*) is darkness, and it is only the manifestation of the Real therein that has illuminated it.' In commentary on these words, al-Shurnūbī says, 'The universe is intrinsically total darkness (i.e. sheer non-existence), because it has no existence in and of itself; rather, what brought it to light (i.e. into existence) is the manifestation of the Real ﷻ therein, namely, a manifestation of [Him] bringing it into existence and making Himself known, not a manifestation of indwelling and modality. In other words, He manifested Himself to it with His entity and said to it, "Be, and it was", and He is able to terminate it now and in the future.' *Ibid.* 79. Thus, what is meant by Him being manifest in creation is not to be understood as Him ﷻ indwelling therein, as this is rationally and textually impossible to attribute to Allah. In fact, no common Muslim believes that Allah can indwell in creation, let alone eminent Sufis like the author.

Imam Ḥāfiẓ al-Suyūṭī says in a work in defence of the Shādhilī Order, 'Amongst the Sufis who have supported the position of declaring those who believe in indwelling (*ḥulūl*) or union (*ittiḥād*) [of the Divine with the creation] to be disbelievers is Ḥāfiẓ Abū Nu'aym al-Aṣfahānī in the beginning of [his work] *al-Ḥilyah*, as previously mentioned, and likewise Qāḍī Nāṣir al-Dīn al-Bayḍāwī, the authority (Imam) in Qur'anic exegesis, jurisprudence, theology, principles of jurisprudence and Sufism. Look at the famous exegesis [by al-Bayḍāwī] and you shall find it filled with Sufism, and he has explicitly mentioned in [the commentary of] *Sūrah al-Mā'idah* that whoever

May Allah bless our master Muhammad, the pure, unblemished, unlettered Prophet and his family with a blessing whereby problems are solved, anxieties are eliminated, harm disappears and difficulties are facilitated, and a blessing that is pleasing to You and him and whereby You are pleased with us, O Lord of the Worlds!

---

believes in indwelling and union [of the Divine with creation] is a disbeliever. Furthermore, Qāḍī 'Iyāḍ says in [his work] *al-Shifā'* (paraphrasing), "The Muslims are in unanimous agreement concerning the disbelief of those who espouse indwelling and whoever claims that the Originator ﷻ indwells in any particular person, as is the opinion of some [so-called] Sufis, esotericists, Christians and the Qarāmiṭah [a heretical sect]." Look how he has ascribed that to some of the Sufis, and these are the extremists amongst them, not all of them (Allah forbid them from that).' The author then goes on to exonerate the Shādhilī Sufis, amongst them the author, from such a heterodoxical belief and refutes this notion. al-Suyūṭī, *Ta'yīd al-ḥaqīqah al-'aliyyah*, 65.

Notes

Made in the USA
Monee, IL
22 December 2021

86844917R00072